Times of Ref

Spring
Devotional

Ruth Gregg

O&U
Onwards & Upwards

Onwards and Upwards Publishers

3 Radfords Turf, Cranbrook, Exeter,
EX5 7DX, United Kingdom.
www.onwardsandupwards.org

First edition, published in the United Kingdom by Onwards and Upwards Publishers (2020).

ISBN:	978-1-78815-538-0
Typeface:	Sabon LT
Graphic design:	LM Graphic Design

Every effort has been made by the author to obtain the necessary permissions to reproduce copyrighted material. If, however, there have been any omissions or errors, please contact the publisher to have these corrected in future reprints and editions.

The views and opinions expressed in this book are the author's own, and do not necessarily represent the views and opinions of Onwards and Upwards Publishers or its staff.

Endorsements

Times of Refreshing does what it says on the tin – it is full to over-flowing with spiritual refreshment. At a time when spiritual attentiveness and soul care can be such easily neglected spiritual disciplines, due to the busy demands made on our lives by so many other things, this spiritually anointed and biblically literate gem of Ruth's is pure gold. It is a collection of inspiring and deeply personal devotionals which come out of a heart which has been captivated by the Father's amazing love and longs for deep personal and national revival – you will certainly meet the Saviour in its pages.

Rev. Daniel Kane
West Presbyterian Church, Ballymena

There are often times in the normal day-to-day hectic schedule of ministry life that you run out of steam and need to have a pit-stop. Sadly, I am on first name terms with a lot of the deli-counter staff and hot food staff all over Ballymena! This also can be said of our walk with God; we can run out of steam and need a pit-stop. In *Times of Refreshing*, Ruth has provided the perfect spiritual pick-me-up – a devotional that can allow us to pause, rest for a while, have a spiritual snack and re-charge our batteries. Better than any meal deal, *Times of Refreshing* will help us run our race and fight our battles. In fact, why don't you get your copy and keep it where you work and make it part of your daily pit-stop routine? Ruth, thank you for this gift. My prayer, like yours, is that many will find essential daily spiritual refreshing as they use *Times of Refreshing*.

Rev. Mark McConnell
Rector, Ballymena Parish Church

There is nothing quite as good for any of us as to spend the first part of the day meditating on the Word of God. As I have read through this beautiful devotional that Ruth has written, I know that many lives will be refreshed and encouraged. Ruth has brought fresh revelation on the Scriptures and nuggets of truth that you can ponder on throughout the day. I highly recommend this book as a tool for anyone who hungers for more of GOD.

Pastor Roy Stewart
Pastor, Celebration House, Ballymena

About the Author

Ruth has been involved in ministry for the past thirty years. She holds a B.D. from Queens University, a Doctorate in Biblical Studies from CLU, has released various print publications, and currently resides in County Antrim, Northern Ireland. She is director of Impact Unlimited Bible College and CTTW, a 24/7 global prayer initiative.

Her passion is to inspire others through writing in a way that is insightful, meaningful and relevant. In the *Times of Refreshing* devotionals, she taps into her experiences as a pastor, teacher, wife and mother of two, to relate poignant stories from real-life experiences.

To contact the author, please write to:

Ruth Gregg
c/o Onwards and Upwards Publishers Ltd.
3 Radfords Turf
Exeter
EX5 7DX

More information about the author can be found on the author's web page:

www.onwardsandupwards.org/ruth-gregg

Foreword by Tommy Stewart

Times of Refreshing is a devotional full of life-changing words of inspiration and encouragement written by Dr Ruth Gregg, drawn from a lifetime of study of God's Word. The devotional has been written to encourage the reader to trust God in every circumstance of life and to give the reader courage each day to step out in faith, believing that God is with them and has good plans for their lives.

I have known Dr Ruth Gregg from our college days when Ruth was studying Theology and I was studying Economics. My earliest impressions were of someone deeply committed to the study of God's Word and to being able to communicate it in such a way that the Word of God came alive in the life of the hearer. Through Ruth's ministry, both as a pastor and a teacher, she has shown herself to be "a worker who does not need to be ashamed and who correctly handles the Word of truth." (2 Tim. 2:15). Her dedication to creating teaching materials for pastors in the 10/40 window and her passion for revival mean that Ruth's writings are filled with great truths, anointed by the Holy Spirit.

If, like me, you have struggled to read and meditate daily on what the Bible has to say, then *Times of Refreshing* will provide you with the opportunity to develop a daily rhythm of reading and mediating on the truth of God's Word.

It is said that it takes twenty-one days to develop a habit. I can think of few better habits that you could develop than creating space each day, with the help of *Times of Refreshing*, to be refreshed by God's Word.

I wonder, can you answer yes to any of the following questions?

- Do you want to have a deeper sense of God's peace?
- Do you want to grow closer to God?
- Do you want to be more like Jesus?
- Do you want to know more of God's Word?
- Do you want to grow in confidence in who you are in Christ?

Then, be assured, *Times of Refreshing* is for you!

Tommy Stewart
Founder/Director, Christians Who Lead

March

March

1

Lonely as a Cloud

Turn to me and be gracious to me, for I am lonely and afflicted. Relieve the troubles of my heart and free me from my anguish.

Psalm 25:16 (ESV)

*D*riving past golden daffodils lining roadside verges on my daily commute, I can't help but burst into recitation of the poem by William Wordsworth:

I wandered lonely as a cloud
That floats on high o'er vales and hills,
When all at once I saw a crowd,
A host, of golden daffodils;
Beside the lake, beneath the trees,
Fluttering and dancing in the breeze.

I remember writing essays based on this poem such as, "Explore the theme of loneliness in William Wordsworth's poem *Daffodils*," or, "What was the poet's state of mind in writing the poem?" *Loneliness.* Even the word sounds sad, doesn't it? Albert Einstein once said:

It is strange to be known so universally and yet to be so lonely.

There is a difference between aloneness and loneliness. As Tim Hansel said:

Loneliness is not the same as being alone. Loneliness is feeling alone ... no matter how many people are around you. It is a feeling of being disconnected, unplugged, left out, isolated.[1]

Loneliness can be experienced when we're alone or when we are completely surrounded by people. It is both ironic and tragic that in a

---

[1]   Tim Hansel; *Through the Wilderness of Loneliness;* David C. Cook Publishers, Elgin, IL (1991); pp.59-60

time when we are more connected technologically than ever, we also see some of the highest recorded rates of loneliness in history.

Do you feel like you are all alone; that no one in the world cares for you? Perhaps you're lonely now. Have you been in a crowded room and felt like you were the only person there? Have you ever cried yourself to sleep because you felt like no one cares? In the Bible David experienced such profound moments of loneliness and cried out in despair. Many Psalms address his deep loneliness. For example:

I am like a pelican of the wilderness: I am like an owl of the desert. I lie awake, and am like a sparrow alone on the housetop.

Psalm 102:6-7 (KJV)

I am full of heaviness: and I looked for some to take pity, but there was none; and for comforters, but I found none.

Psalm 69:20 (KJV)

I look for someone to come and help me, but no one gives me a passing thought! No one will help me; no one cares a bit what happens to me.

Psalm 142:4 (NLT)

There are many lonely people today. You may be lonely, but you're never alone. Jesus promised never to leave us.[2] If no one else understands, He does. If everybody else fails you, He will not. Jesus says:

"I am with you always, to the very end of the age."

Matthew 28:20b (NIV)

It is interesting to note that the word 'lonely' is never used in the New Testament to describe people, only places. In Christ we have constant companionship. When you see the familiar trumpet-shaped springtime blooms, cherish the presence of Christ with you daily and reach out to someone in your community who is 'lonely as a cloud'.

---

[2] See Hebrews 13:5

2

Focus on Our Feathered Friends

Look at the birds of the air, for they neither sow nor reap nor gather into barns; yet your heavenly Father feeds them. Are you not of more value than they?

Matthew 6:26 (NKJV)

Birds are amazing creatures when you take into account their migratory capacity, their variety of birdsong, their nest-building skills and their marvellous aerodynamic soaring and swooping in the sky.

Jesus tells us to look at the birds of the air. They do not plant or harvest crops, yet our heavenly Father feeds them. Each new day their needs are met. Jesus wants us to learn a lesson from this and, whenever we see a wild bird, to stop, look and remember the implicit trust it has in God's provision, then reset our thinking to trust God to provide for us. As the poem says:

Said the robin to the sparrow:
"I should really like to know
Why these anxious human beings
Rush about and worry so."
Said the sparrow to the robin:
"Friend, I think that it must be
That they have no heavenly Father,
Such as cares for you and me."

It has been quipped, "If Worry were a sport, I might not win the gold, silver or bronze medal, but I would definitely make it to the Olympics!" If God takes care of the birds, will He not take care of you as well? How much more does God care for His children, created in His own image?

Start looking at the birds and stop worrying.

3

Worry is Worldly

"But seek first His kingdom and His righteousness, and all these things will be added to you."

Matthew 6:33 (NASB)

The context of this verse is the Sermon on the Mount – one of the most extensive documentations of the preaching and teaching of Jesus. In this section of it,[3] Jesus addresses the common questions each of us face in order to survive: *how am I going to pay the bills?* etc. In essence, Jesus cautions us not to worry about these human concerns or obligations, and instead we are to place our greatest priority on seeking God's Kingdom.

> *Therefore do not worry or be anxious (perpetually uneasy, distracted), saying, 'What are we going to eat?' or 'What are we going to drink?' or 'What are we going to wear?' For the [pagan] Gentiles eagerly seek all these things; [but do not worry,] for your heavenly Father knows that you need them. But first and most importantly seek (aim at, strive after) His kingdom and His righteousness [His way of doing and being right – the attitude and character of God], and all these things will be given to you also.*

Matthew 6:31-33 (AMP)

Worry is worldly. Shouldn't the Christian live differently than those who have no relationship with God? Yes. Notice the word "But" – "But seek first His kingdom..." In other words, instead of being anxious and worrying, there is a better way. Rather than being like the pagans who are concerned only about their physical needs, the citizens of the Kingdom of Heaven should be concerned about and seek after the things of God. The word "seek" means 'to actively pursue' or 'to go after'. It's

---

[3]   Matthew 6:25-34

in the present tense and thus implies seeking continuously. In order to seek the kingdom, you must first seek the King and His rule, and over your entire life.

"...and all these things will be given to you also." Jesus had already said, "...for your heavenly Father knows that you need all these things." Isn't that beautiful? There is no need to worry or stress. We don't have to worry about any of "these things" because we have a sovereign Father in heaven who cares for us.

4

Have You Ever Seen a Worldly Lily?

"And why are you worried about clothing? Observe how the lilies of the field grow; they do not toil nor do they spin, yet I say to you that not even Solomon in all his glory clothed himself like one of these. But if God so clothes the grass of the field, which is alive today and tomorrow is thrown into the furnace, will He not much more clothe you? You of little faith!"

Matthew 6:28-30 (NASB)

I remember back to primary school where we had a nature table. Each child was encouraged to go foraging for wildflowers and present their specimens to the class. Living in the countryside, I was spoilt for choice. Jesus draws our attention to these wildflowers. The verb "observe" is a strong word. It means more than just a mere casual glance. It means to 'really look' and wonder at the intricate and delicate construction of petals and leaves.

In essence Jesus is saying, "Have you ever seen a worried lily? Of course not. God provides every necessity for their existence and they want for nothing. They grow and are clothed by God while simply resting and basking in the sunshine of God's love. And when God clothes them, they look even more glorious than King Solomon, the richest king who ever lived."

Life can be overwhelming at times, especially in today's ever-increasing political and economic uncertainty. But Jesus points out that worry is futile; it is a waste of time and accomplishes nothing.

"And which of you by being anxious can add a single hour to his span of life?"

Matthew 6:27 (ESV)

Trust God to meet your needs. He will sustain you. Focus on the flora and fauna around you today and learn the lesson of divine dependence in every detail. If God is so concerned with a flower, how much more concerned is God for His people?

> *"For I know the plans I have for you," declares the LORD, "plans to prosper you and not to harm you, plans to give you hope and a future."*
>
> *Jeremiah 29:11 (NIV)*

5

How Deeply are You Rooted?

Therefore as you have received Christ Jesus the Lord, so walk in Him, having been firmly rooted and now being built up in Him and established in your faith, just as you were instructed, and overflowing with gratitude.

Colossians 2:6-7 (NASB)

Notice the words "having been firmly rooted" and "now being built up in Him". Both being 'firmly rooted' and being 'built up' are important but the second depends on the first. The building up of our lives depends on a proper foundation or, in the analogy of a tree, having well established roots. A plant can only grow upward to the extent that its roots grow downward and are established.

Let us pause to consider our root system. The Scriptures warn us of what happens to those who are not deeply rooted in Christ. Notice what Jesus taught about this subject:

"But since they have no root, they last only a short time. When trouble or persecution comes because of the word, they quickly fall away."

Mark 4:17 (NIV)

The lesson above, which was taught by Christ in the 'Parable of the Sower' shows us the importance of being deeply rooted in the word of our Lord.

In the Far East, there is a tree called the Chinese bamboo tree. This remarkable tree is different from most in that it doesn't grow in the usual fashion. While most trees grow steadily over a period of years, the Chinese bamboo tree breaks convention. Like any plant, growth of the Chinese Bamboo Tree requires nurturing – water, fertile soil, sunshine. In its first year, we see no visible signs of activity. In the second year, again, no growth above the soil. The third, the fourth, still nothing. Our patience is tested and we begin to wonder if our efforts (caring, water, etc.) will ever be rewarded. Finally, in the fifth year – behold, a miracle! We experience growth. The Chinese Bamboo Tree grows eighty feet in just six weeks! Did the Chinese Bamboo Tree lie dormant for four years only to grow exponentially in the fifth? Or, was the little tree growing underground, developing a root system strong enough to support its potential for outward growth in the fifth year and beyond? The answer is, of course, clear. Had the tree not developed a strong unseen foundation, it could not have sustained its life as it grew. The same principle is true for us.

The Bible shares the benefits of being rooted through the prophet Jeremiah, who expressed one of the most beautiful analogies in the Old Testament, comparing the faith-filled person with a strong, flourishing tree:

> *Blessed is the man who trusts in the Lord, whose hope is the Lord. He is like a tree planted beside waters, that stretches out its roots to the stream. It fears not the heat when it comes, its leaves stay green. In the year of drought it shows no distress, but still bears fruit.*
>
> *Jeremiah 17:7-9 (NABRE)*

So let's stretch out our roots. When we grow deep in Christ, we can live tall.

6

Will They Know Us by Our Love?

"By this all men will know that you are My disciples, if you have love for one another."

John 13:35 (NASB)

*T*he authenticating mark of our Christianity before an unbelieving world is our love for other believers. Jesus affirmed this through the words in today's reading. Notice Jesus did not say that people will know that we are His disciples by wearing our Christian T-shirts or a WWJD bracelet, or having a fish symbol on our car, but rather if we love one another. Will they know us by our love? He didn't say they would know us by our dress code or our doctrinal differences or dogmatic opinions – they would know us by our love.

In the early 3rd century, the church father Tertullian wrote:

It is mainly the deeds of a love so noble that lead many to put a brand upon us! 'See,' they say, 'how they love one another ... see how they are ready even to die for one another.'

From the very beginning, God's plan was to develop a people that reflected His character. And what is His character? Love.

For this is the message you have heard from the beginning: we should love one another.

1 John 3:11 (HCSB)

Mother Teresa, when asked how she had accomplished such great things in her life, said this:

None of us can do anything great on our own, but we can all do a small thing with great love.

Paul told us to clothe ourselves with love. When writing to the church members at Colosse he said:

Make allowance for each other's faults, and forgive anyone who offends you. Remember, the Lord forgave you, so you must forgive others. Above all, clothe yourselves with love, which binds us all together in perfect harmony.

Colossians 3:13-14 (NLT)

Or as another translation phrases that final verse:

And regardless of what else you put on, wear love. It's your basic, all-purpose garment. Never be without it.

Colossians 3:14 (MSG)

The question that hangs in the air for us is this: what do others experience when they meet us? Do they encounter love? None of us ever fully lives up to this challenge, but that doesn't mean we need to despair. Jesus called us His disciples, which means 'learners'. A Christian is someone who is learning to love, to be more considerate, compassionate, caring, courteous and charitable. That requires us to be patient with each other as we journey in this process and to bear with one another.

Be patient with each other, making allowance for each other's faults because of your love.

Ephesians 4:2 (TLB)

7

Beauty for Ashes

...to give unto them beauty for ashes, the oil of joy for mourning, the garment of praise for the spirit of heaviness; that they might be called trees of righteousness, the planting of the Lord, that he might be glorified.

Isaiah 61:3 (KJV)

*I*saiah 61 contains the manifesto of the Messiah. In Luke 4:16-22 Jesus stood up in the synagogue in Nazareth and spoke about the ministry God had given Him. He quoted from Isaiah 61, relating how God had anointed Him, and telling what that anointing was to accomplish. Verse 3 speaks of how God wants to bless your life with beauty, joy and praise. Look at the contrast: ashes, mourning, the spirit of despair – beauty, the oil of joy, the garment of praise.

The Bible says that He will give us beauty for ashes. In Bible times it was the custom for the people of that day in great times of difficulty to lie in ashes. For example, if you had a problem in your life, you would sit down in a pile of ashes. When we think about ashes, we think about the remains after a fire has gone out. Ashes are nothing more than the remains of something that once was. Ashes may represent your life if you are grieving your past; grieving past relationships; grieving past memories; grieving past moments of blessing and are dreaming of 'what used to be'! But watch this! The Hebrew word for ashes is *epher* and the Hebrew word for beauty is *pheer*. Just move the e and you have a new word. Just as quickly as it takes for you to move one letter, God can turn around your circumstances. God can transform your trying situation. God is ready to show Himself strong on your behalf in the midst of hopeless situations.

You may be burnt by life's experiences, but God can "restore ... the years ... the locust hath eaten"[4].

---

[4]   Joel 2:25 (KJV)

He raises the poor from the dust and lifts the needy from the ash heap.

Psalm 113:7 (ESV)

The world spends billions of pounds each year trying to look more beautiful, but God gives us a beauty that cannot be bought, a radiance, a glow for those who know Him.

8

The Oil of Joy

...to give unto them beauty for ashes, the oil of joy for mourning, the garment of praise for the spirit of heaviness; that they might be called trees of righteousness, the planting of the Lord, that he might be glorified.

Isaiah 61:3 (KJV)

The Bible says that He will give us the oil of joy for mourning. In Psalm 30 we read the words:

You have turned my mourning into joyful dancing. You have taken away my clothes of mourning and clothed me with joy, that I might sing praises to you and not be silent. O Lord my God, I will give you thanks forever!

Psalm 30:11-12 (NLT)

In the same Psalm it says:

Weeping may last through the night, but joy comes with the morning.

Psalm 30:5 (NLT)

God wants you and me to experience the oil of joy. He wants songs of joy and victory to be sung in the camp of the godly.

Shouts of joy and victory resound in the tents of the righteous.

Psalm 118:15 (NIV)

Is there joy in your tent? Is joy resounding from your tent? What does your joy-meter show?

The Jewish Encyclopaedia tells us that no language has as many words for joy and rejoicing as does the language of the Old Testament Hebrew. And that's because God's people were meant to be a joyful people. For example:

For you shall go out in joy and be led forth in peace.

Isaiah 55:12 (ESV)

...the joy of the LORD is your strength.

Nehemiah 8:10 (NKJV)

In Thy presence is fullness of joy.

Psalm 16:1 (KJV)

Rejoice in the Lord always: and again I say, Rejoice.

Philippians 4:4 (KJV)

Peter says:

Though you have not seen him, you love him; and even though you do not see him now, you believe in him and are filled with an inexpressible and glorious joy, for you are receiving the end result of your faith, the salvation of your souls.

1 Peter 1:8 (NIV)

Joy is not dependent upon your circumstances; it is a by-product of relationship with Jesus and a Spirit-filled life. Jesus told us in John 15:

"These things I have spoken to you, that My joy may remain in you, and that your joy may be full."

John 15:11 (NKJV)

May we experience the oil of joy.

This is the day the LORD has made;
let us rejoice and be glad in it.

Psalm 118:24 (ESV)

9

Put on the Garment of Praise

...to give unto them beauty for ashes, the oil of joy for mourning, the garment of praise for the spirit of heaviness; that they might be called trees of righteousness, the planting of the LORD, that he might be glorified.

Isaiah 61:3 (KJV)

Or, "The mantle of praise instead of a spirit of fainting."[5] The Bible says that He will also give us the garment of praise for the spirit of heaviness. Let me try to paint a picture for you because the word for "heaviness" is used on other occasions and in other contexts in the Old Testament.

It is applied to a lamp that's about to go out in Isaiah 42:3:

A bruised reed he will not break, and a smoking flax he will not quench.

Isaiah 42:3 (NKJV)

Smoking flax is the translation of our word for "heaviness". It is like a candle going out, or when the flame is low. The same word is also used in 1 Samuel 3:2 of Eli's eyesight being dimmed or dulled – vision is dimmed and everything looks darker. It's also used in Leviticus 13:39 of a faint or pale colour in the instruction given to the priests over deciding whether a leprous spot has been cleansed or not.

So "spirit of heaviness" is when you are off-colour, your vision is dimmed, your outlook dark and your flame is low. But God gives us the garment of praise. Praise is so powerful. It not only honours God but it silences the enemy. When you choose to magnify the Lord you immediately minimise the lies of the enemy. No wonder then that David declared:

---

[5] NASB

I will bless the LORD at all times;
His praise shall continually be in my mouth.

Psalm 34:1 (NKJV)

Through worship you are reminded that God is bigger than the situation you face. So no matter where you find yourself today, put on the garment of praise for the spirit of heaviness.

Let us continually offer the sacrifice of praise to God, that is, the fruit of our lips, giving thanks to His name.

Hebrews 13:15 (NKJV)

Fill your day with praise. Wrap yourself up in it.

10

Wait

Wait for the LORD;
Be strong and let your heart take courage;
Yes, wait for the LORD.

Psalm 27:14 (NASB)

Wait for and confidently expect the LORD;
Be strong and let your heart take courage;
Yes, wait for and confidently expect the LORD.

Psalm 27:14 (AMP)

*S*o many of the Psalms of David in the Bible were written during times of deep personal distress. Yet always, by the grace of God, David came to see that his help was of the Lord, that his strength was not of himself, that his deliverance would not be due to his ingenuity, but the Lord would deliver him. So he says in Psalm 27:

I had fainted, unless I had believed to see the goodness of the
Lord in the land of the living.

Psalm 27:13 (KJV)

In the next verse he concludes with a final word of counsel which is relevant to every one of us, no matter the trials we face today. That word is this: "Wait on the Lord."

Spurgeon, in his sermon 'Brave Waiting' said:

That word, 'wait', is so exceedingly comprehensive that I quite
despair of bringing out every shade of its meaning. Rightly
understood waiting is active as well as passive, energetic as
well as patient and to wait upon the Lord necessitates as much
holy courage as warring and fighting with His enemies.

What do we mean, then, by "wait on the Lord"? Here are some examples of its meaning. We wait on the Lord:

- as a needy beggar waits for alms at the rich man's door – only in God is there a supply for the deep poverty of our souls;
- as a learner waits for instruction – the disciple waits at his Master's feet and is eager to drink in what He says;
- as a servant waits upon his lord – a true servant is anxious to know what his master wishes him to do and when he once knows it, he is happy to undertake it and carry it through;
- as a traveller waiting for the directions of his guide – God's hand is to steer our course ("This is the way. Walk in it.");
- as a child waits upon a parent – our children can seldom be accused of having small expectations with reference to us; they expect that their needs will be met and do not waste time in anxiety.

Wait on the Lord: be of good courage,
and He shall strengthen thine heart:
wait, I say, on the Lord.

Psalm 27:14 (KJV)

May His grace enable us daily to say:

I wait for the LORD, my soul does wait,
and in His Word do I hope.

Psalm 130:5 (NASB)

11

Do This with Gentleness and Respect

But in your hearts revere Christ as Lord. Always be prepared to give an answer to everyone who asks you to give the reason for the hope that you have. But do this with gentleness and respect...

1 Peter 3:15 (NIV)

*W*hen people first hear the word 'apologetics', they typically think of our modern use of the word apology. They often conclude that the task of apologetics is apologising for the Christian faith as if to say we are sorry for what we believe. However, the word apologetics derives from the Greek word *apologia*, which means 'to give an answer' or 'to make a defence'. Apologetics is not an apology, it's an answer – a defence of what we believe.

Always be prepared to give an answer [apologia] to everyone...

1 Peter 3:15 (NIV)

We are to be ready to make a defence for the hope that is in us, but notice that Peter calls us to do it with gentleness and respect. It is not only what we say that is important, but how we say it. There is no room for arrogance, a know-it-all attitude or ramming our beliefs down someone's throat. You can't argue people into the Kingdom of God. Rather, Paul told us that we are to "speak the truth in love"[6]. We are called not only to speak the truth but to do so in love.

Paul also told us:

Be wise in the way you act toward outsiders; make the most of every opportunity. Let your conversation be always full of

---

[6] Ephesians 4:15 (NLT)

grace, seasoned with salt, so that you may know how to answer everyone.

Colossians 4:5-6 (NIV)

People need to hear the gospel – to hear that God loves them, Christ died for them and that they can have eternal life.

'Everyone who calls on the name of the Lord will be saved.' How, then, can they call on the one they have not believed in? And how can they believe in the one of whom they have not heard? And how can they hear without someone preaching to them?

Romans 10:13-14 (NIV)

God has called us all to reach people as we live out our everyday lives, to help those around us find and experience His grace. Paul reminds us:

...we are Christ's ambassadors; God is making his appeal through us.

2 Corinthians 5:20 (NLT)

Let's remember as we witness to do so with gentleness and respect, to speak the truth in love and allow our conversation to be full of grace.

12

Do You Have Beautiful Feet?

How beautiful on the mountains are the feet of those who bring good news, who proclaim peace, who bring good tidings, who proclaim salvation, who say to Zion, "Your God reigns!"

Isaiah 52:7 (NIV)

Have you ever wondered how far you walk in a day? A year? A lifetime? Apparently, the average person takes around 7,500 steps per day. Thus the average person, with an average stride, living until eighty years old, will walk the distance of about 110,000 miles. To put this in perspective, the circumference of the earth is 24,901 miles at the equator. This means that you would walk *five* times around the earth! That's quite a distance.

The Bible talks about our feet and calls them beautiful. How many of us have thought of feet as being beautiful? The Bible says that the feet of those who bring the gospel of Jesus Christ are "beautiful".

In Romans 10:15, Paul borrows from the language of Isaiah 52:7 and relates it to the ultimate good news message.

How then will they call on Him in whom they have not believed? How will they believe in Him whom they have not heard? And how will they hear without a preacher? How will they preach unless they are sent? Just as it is written, "How beautiful are the feet of those who bring good news of good things!"

Romans 10:14-15 (NASB)

The words "preacher" and "preach" today make us immediately think of pulpits. Actually, the word "preach" simply means to proclaim, to make known! In centuries past, before the invention of the wire cable and the printing press, there were messengers who ran on foot with important news. These envoys delivered the news in person. In biblical times people relied on these heralds who would bring news or a message from important dignitaries. The recipients would be anxious to know if the news was good or bad.

Our message is thankfully good news. The bringers of good news provide a message that gives peace within and without. As the angel put it in Luke 2:10:

> *"I bring you good news of great joy which will be for all the people."*
>
> *Luke 2:10 (NASB)*

Have your feet brought good news to someone recently? Let's go as messengers of the Good News.

13

Christ the Desire of All Nations

And the desire of all nations shall come.

Haggai 2:7

What a beautiful description of our Lord: "the desire of all nations"… Revelation 7 graphically tells us:

After these things I looked, and behold, a great multitude which no one could count, from every nation and all tribes and peoples and tongues, standing before the throne and before the Lamb, clothed in white robes, and palm branches were in their hands; and they cry out with a loud voice, saying, "Salvation to our God who sits on the throne, and to the Lamb." And all the angels were standing around the throne and around the elders and the four living creatures; and they fell on their faces before the throne and worshiped God, saying, "Amen, blessing and glory and wisdom and thanksgiving and honour and power and might, be to our God forever and ever. Amen."

Revelation 7:9-12 (NASB)

Let us remember those who are reaching into the nations with the life-changing gospel. God says in Psalm 2:

Ask of me, and I will make the nations your heritage,
and the ends of the earth your possession.

Psalm 2:8 (ESV)

Isaiah 56:7 states:

…these I will bring to my holy mountain and give them joy in my house of prayer. Their burnt offerings and sacrifices will be accepted on my altar; for my house will be called a house of prayer for all nations.

Isaiah 56:7 (NIV)

May the nations know the One who is the Desire of All Nations! God's heart is for nations.

> *Declare his glory among the nations,*
> *his marvellous deeds among all peoples.*

Psalm 96:3 (NIVUK)

> *Clap your hands, all you nations;*
> *shout to God with cries of joy.*

Psalm 47:1 (NIVUK)

> *God be gracious to us and bless us,*
> *And cause His face to shine upon us – Selah.*
> *That Your way may be known on the earth,*
> *Your salvation among all nations.*
> *Let the peoples praise You, O God;*
> *Let all the peoples praise You.*
> *Let the nations be glad and sing for joy...*

Psalm 67:1-4 (NASB)

> *"Go therefore and make disciples of all the nations, baptizing them in the name of the Father and the Son and the Holy Spirit, teaching them to observe all that I commanded you; and lo, I am with you always, even to the end of the age."*

Matthew 28:19-20 (NKJV)

14

It is High Time

Do this, knowing the time, that it is already the hour for you to awaken from sleep; for now salvation is nearer to us than when we believed. The night is almost gone, and the day is near.

Romans 13:11-12 (NASB)

o what? In context Paul is referring to what he has just emphasised. We are called to love richly and live right. Knowing the time is important. Christians are addressed as those who know the seasons, who discern the signs of the times. The word for "time" is *kairos*, also translated as "opportunity". *Kairos* is not so much a succession of minutes (Greek *chronos*), but a period of opportunity. That's why we are told to redeem the time.

Let's check out other translations for insight into this verse.

You know how late it is; time is running out. Wake up.

Romans 13:11-12 (TLB)

Time is running out!

The night is about over, dawn is about to break. Be up and awake to what God is doing!

Romans 13:11-12 (MSG)

Be up and awake to what God is doing!

It is time to wake up to reality. Every day brings God's salvation nearer. The night is nearly over, the day has almost dawned.

Romans 13:11-12 (JBP)

It is time to wake up to reality!

And that, knowing the time, that now it is high time to awake out of sleep: for now is our salvation nearer than when we believed. The night is far spent, the day is at hand.

Romans 13:11-12 (KJV)

Sleep is *hupnos* in the original Greek. It is the source of our English words 'hypnotic', 'hypnosis', etc. Let's shake off that hypnotic state. It's not time to hit the snooze button. It's time to be alert, awake and aware of the opportunities God has given us. Let's make each day count and impact our communities. As Jesus said:

I must work the works of Him that sent Me, while it is day: the night comes when no man can work.

John 9:4 (KJV)

15

External Chaos, Internal Peace

"Peace I leave with you; My peace I give to you; not as the world gives do I give to you. Do not let your heart be troubled, nor let it be fearful."

John 14:27 (NASB)

*T*he hymn-writer Joseph Scriven wrote, "Oh, what peace we often forfeit, oh what needless pain we bear." Isn't that true? Just hours before Jesus was crucified, He was concerned for the peace of his followers. His work in the next twenty-four hours following these words would make that peace a reality. The message for us is this: in the midst of external chaos you can have internal peace.

His peace is a gift to us. We can't earn it. We can't buy it. We simply receive it.

"I am leaving you with a gift – peace of mind and heart! And the peace I give isn't fragile like the peace the world gives. So don't be troubled or afraid."

John 14:27 (TLB)

Christ is the exclusive source of peace. Seven hundred years before He was born, the prophet Isaiah foretold that He would be called the Prince of Peace.[7]

[Jesus] said unto the sea, 'Peace! Be still!' And the wind ceased, and there was a great calm.

Mark 4:39 (ESV)

He is the source of peace and it is out of this world. The world cannot give it. "…not as the world gives do I give to you." This isn't a pseudo peace; this is perfect peace.

---

[7] See Isaiah 9:6

"Peace I leave with you; My [perfect] peace I give to you; not as the world gives do I give to you. Do not let your heart be troubled, nor let it be afraid. [Let My perfect peace calm you in every circumstance and give you courage and strength for every challenge.]"

John 14:27 (AMP)

Jesus did not want our hearts to be troubled or fearful. Whatever circumstances of life we face, we can have this wonderful tranquillity, this sense of calmness and confidence in God. Reread the words, "Let My perfect peace calm you in every circumstance and give you courage and strength for every challenge." It's a peace that will calm the heart in every situation, in every circumstance, in every storm of life. Or as Paul said:

May the Lord of peace Himself give you His peace at all times and in every situation.

2 Thessalonians 3:16 (NLT)

16

When Life Throws You a Curveball, Still Make a Home Run!

We are hard-pressed on every side, yet not crushed; we are perplexed, but not in despair; persecuted, but not forsaken; struck down, but not destroyed.

2 Corinthians 4:8-9 (NKJV)

In the world ye shall have tribulation.

John 16:33 (KJV)

*Y*ou're going to have trouble! Jesus stated, "In the world, ye shall have tribulation." But He didn't stop there. He added, "But be of good cheer." Why? "I have overcome the world."[8] The psalmist phrased it:

Many are the afflictions of the righteous, but God delivereth him out of them all!

Psalm 34:19 (KJV)

Paul testified:

- we are pressed on every side by troubles, but we are not crushed;
- we are perplexed, but not driven to despair;
- we are hunted down, but never abandoned by God;
- we get knocked down, but we are not destroyed.

PRESSED/PRESSURISED

We are hard pressed on every side, but not crushed.

2 Corinthians 4:8a (NKJV)

---

[8]   John 16:33 (KJV)

PERPLEXED

> *[We are] perplexed, but not in despair.*
>
> *2 Corinthians 4:8b (NKJV)*

The verb here, *aporeomai*, means 'to be at one's wits' end'. Life has a way of throwing us a curveball now and then.

PERSECUTED

> *[We are] persecuted, but not abandoned.*
>
> *2 Corinthians 4:9a (NKJV)*

In his first letter to the Corinthian church, Paul describes his situation:

> *A wide door for effective work has opened to me, and there are many adversaries.*
>
> *1 Corinthians 16:9 (ESV)*

PUNCHED

> *[We are] struck down, but not destroyed.*
>
> *2 Corinthians 4:9b (NKJV)*

J.B. Phillips offers us this memorable paraphrase:

> *We may be knocked down, but we are never knocked out!*
>
> *2 Corinthians 4:9b (JBP)*

Though Paul was pressed, perplexed, persecuted and punched, he also finished his sentence and confidently stated what He was:

- not crushed;
- not driven to despair;
- never abandoned by God;
- not destroyed.

From my experience playing baseball on the Wii with my children over the years, I have noticed everyone dislikes curveballs, but I have also learned that with the right attitude you can make a home run! That's what Paul did with what life threw at him and we can learn from his attitude. When life throws you a curveball, still make a home run!

17

God Sees the Lid

*I declare the end from the beginning, and from long ago what
is not yet done, saying: My plan will take place, and I will do
all My will.*

Isaiah 46:10 (HCSB)

*H*ave you ever tried to put together a jigsaw puzzle with at least
a thousand pieces? That has been considered a winter sport in
our home over the years. At first glance into the large box of
tiny freeform pieces, it's hard to imagine they will form a picture. Some
indeed are really laborious, for example, the one of 101 Dalmatians!

We usually undertake the task by looking for the corner and border
pieces. From the corner pieces we can build a framework for the entire
puzzle. Likewise in life, unless we start correctly with the correct
Corner(stone),[9] our attempts to solve our puzzle will be futile. Jesus must
get pre-eminence. Following on, the straight edges in the jigsaw of our
lives are the boundaries God has set in place in His Word. This gives
structure and cohesion to our lives.

Thankfully, the full picture of the completed puzzle is always on the
box-top and God sees the lid. He knows how to put all the pieces of our
lives together, which means we don't have to struggle but simply
surrender to His plan and trust Him.

Trust in the LORD with all your heart;
do not depend on your own understanding.
Seek His will in all you do,
and He will show you which path to take.

Proverbs 3:5-6 (NLT)

As we trust Him, piece by piece of the jigsaw is put into place. I can't
think of a better way to solve a jigsaw puzzle than by letting the puzzle's

---

[9]   See Ephesians 2:20

creator tell me where to interlock the pieces of life. Gradually life's landscape begins to make sense.

It is inevitable that at some point in putting a jigsaw together we will try to put a wrong piece in the wrong place. No matter how much we force the wrong piece into the wrong place it will never fit and if we get it in, it will knock all the other pieces out of place. Don't force what God has not endorsed. Simply return to God's plan knowing each piece is strategic and part of the box top, carefully created by an all-knowing, all-wise and all-loving God. He is the one who has planned all of our days and therefore He knows what's best for us. Remember, He sees the lid!

18

Really and Unquestionably Free

So Jesus said to those Jews who had believed in Him, If you abide in My word [hold fast to My teachings and live in accordance with them], you are truly My disciples. And you will know the Truth, and the Truth will set you free ... So if the Son liberates you [makes you free men], then you are really and unquestionably free.

John 8:31-32,36 (AMPC)

*J*esus, at the onset of his ministry, read from Isaiah 61 saying, "The Spirit of the Lord is on me, because he has anointed me to proclaim good news to the poor. He has sent me to proclaim freedom for the prisoners and recovery of sight for the blind, to set the oppressed free." [10]

As we turn in faith to Jesus, we are liberated and can repeat the words of Charles Wesley's hymn:

Long my imprisoned spirit lay
*   fast bound in sin and nature's night.*
Thine eye diffused a quickening ray,
*   I woke – the dungeon flamed with light!*
My chains fell off, my heart was free;
*   I rose, went forth, and followed Thee.*

The source of our freedom is Christ. And you will know the Truth, and the Truth will set you free. He is the personification of Truth.

Jesus said to him, "I am the way, the truth, and the life."

John 14:6 (NKJV)

His Word is Truth.

---

[10] Luke 4:18 (NIV)

"Sanctify them by Your truth. Your word is truth."

John 17:17 (NKJV)

The scope of our freedom is "really and unquestionably free".

We are free. … Stand fast, therefore, in the liberty wherewith Christ hath made us free, and be not entangled again with the yoke of bondage.

Galatians 4:31; 5:1 (KJV)

We are free indeed. Christ made us really and unquestionably free. But it is important that we continue/abide in His Word so that our minds are constantly enlightened to the Truth and we can experience the reality of living in the Truth, renouncing the lies of the enemy and announcing that we are free indeed.

We are free!

19

Exhibiting Goodness

*But a certain Samaritan, as he journeyed, came where he was:
and when he saw him, he had compassion on him.*

Luke 10:33

*H*ow do we exhibit goodness in daily life? Check out the
character of the good Samaritan.

*Jesus replied and said, "A man was going down from
Jerusalem to Jericho, and fell among robbers, and they
stripped him and beat him, and went away leaving him half
dead. And by chance a priest was going down on that road,
and when he saw him, he passed by on the other side. Likewise
a Levite also, when he came to the place and saw him, passed
by on the other side. But a Samaritan, who was on a journey,
came upon him; and when he saw him, he felt compassion,
and came to him and bandaged up his wounds, pouring oil
and wine on them; and he put him on his own beast, and
brought him to an inn and took care of him. On the next day
he took out two denarii and gave them to the innkeeper and
said, 'Take care of him; and whatever more you spend, when
I return I will repay you.' Which of these three do you think
proved to be a neighbour to the man who fell into the robbers'
hands?" And he said, "The one who showed mercy toward
him." Then Jesus said to him, "Go and do the same."*

Luke 10:30-37 (NASB)

How did he merit the title "good"? What was different about him?
What did he do that the others didn't?

We have the thugs in the story. There was nothing good about them.
They were the ones who stripped the man... wounded him... departed
from him leaving him half-dead. We have the passing priest and Levite.
They passed by on the other side. They were both too busy in religious

service. They lived a lifestyle of avoidance and kept everyone at arm's length. Theirs was an apathetic attitude of non-involvement. How many times do we pass by someone? Then there was the Samaritan.

But a certain Samaritan, as he journeyed, came where he was: and when he saw him, he had compassion on him.

Luke 10:33 (KJV)

He saw the man... he stopped... he showed compassion... he smoothed his wounds... he sacrificed... he spared no expense...

He didn't know how long the injured man would be laid up, but because the text said the attack left him "half dead", it could be a prolonged stay. It didn't matter. He took personal responsibility for this victim in need. This was the man described as good. He was willing to cross social barriers. He was willing to give up personal comfort and be inconvenienced. Jesus' instruction to us is simple, yet profound:

"Go and do likewise."

Luke 10:37 (NKJV)

20

Birdsong in Spring

I will sing to the LORD all my life;
I will sing praise to my God as long as I live.

Psalm 104:33 (NIV)

I awaken regularly to the spring dawn chorus as the birds showcase their vocal talent; some melodious, some rather repetitive. Each species has its own signature song, its own theme tune. Today one particularly loquacious thrush was very vocal outside my window. Birdsong has inspired poets and composers through the centuries. Grieg, Ravel and Vaughan Williams have been so fascinated by the melody of blackbirds, skylarks, nightingales and doves that they have turned their calls into music. Vivaldi composed the famous 'Goldfinch' concerto. Girolamo Frescobaldi's 'Capriccio sopra Cucho' is a testimony to the charms of the cuckoo. The most famous example of a cuckoo call in music is in Beethoven's *Pastoral Symphony*, where at the end of the second movement, the 'Scene by the Brook', there is a cadenza for three birds: a flute imitates a nightingale, an oboe the quail and a pair of clarinets for the cuckoo.

A typical songbird belts out its song between 1,000 and 2,500 times per day. How about us? The Bible speaks of us "singing and making melody with your heart to the Lord"[11]. The Bible contains over four hundred references to singing and fifty direct commands to sing. The longest book of the Bible, the Psalms, is a book of songs. Joyful, exuberant, heartfelt singing was evidenced in the daily life of the Psalmist. He declared:

I will praise God's name in song and glorify Him with thanksgiving.

Psalm 69:30 (NIV)

---

[11] Ephesians 5:19 (AMP)

I will sing of the LORD's great love forever...

Psalm 89:1 (NIV)

I will sing to the LORD,
  because He has dealt bountifully with me.

Psalm 13:6 (AMPC)

How good it is to sing praises to our God,
  how pleasant and fitting to praise Him!

Psalm 147:1 (NIV)

He invites us to join in.

Come before His presence with singing.

Psalm 100:2 (NKJV)

Come, let us sing for joy to the LORD;
  let us shout aloud to the Rock of our salvation.
Let us come before Him with thanksgiving
  and extol him with music and song.

Psalm 95:1 (NIV)

O sing unto the Lord a new song:
  sing unto the Lord, all the earth.

Psalm 96:1 (KJV)

Let sighing flee away and singing fill the air. When you hear the birds singing their hearts out, remember to sing your own song of salvation. What is the song you are singing today?

21

Eden Spring Water

How precious is your unfailing love, O God!
All humanity finds shelter in the shadow of your wings.
You feed them from the abundance of your own house,
letting them drink from your river of delights.

Psalm 36:7-8 (NLT)

*I*f I asked you to name some rivers found in the Bible, it is probable that you would refer to the Euphrates, the Nile or the Jordan, as they are connected with significant biblical events. But did you know there is a river in the Bible called God's "river of delights"? It is mentioned in Psalm 36:8 where God allows us to drink from "the river of delights".

The word "delights" stood out to me, and when I looked up the original Hebrew I learned that the Hebrew word is *eden*. Does that sound familiar? It is the same word as is translated "Eden" in Genesis, only here in verse 8 it is in the plural. We know that in the beginning the garden was perfect and encompassed every kind of provision of which Adam and Eve could ever have needed. See how the Message Bible translates today's verses:

How exquisite your love, O God! How eager we are to run
under your wings, to eat our fill at the banquet you spread as
you fill our tankards with Eden spring water.

Psalm 36:7-8 (MSG)

Drinking from His river of delights is the only basis for lasting satisfaction. The Psalmist said:

As a deer pants for flowing streams,
so pants my soul for you, O God.
My soul thirsts for God,
for the living God.

Psalm 42:1-2 (ESV)

My soul thirsts for you; my flesh faints for you,
*   as in a dry and weary land where there is no water.*

Psalm 63:1 (ESV)

God in His extravagant and unfailing love allows us access to drink from the river of His delights.

In Isaiah 55:1, He invites us:

Come, all you who are thirsty, come to the waters.

Isaiah 55:1 (NIV)

Jesus says:

"If anyone thirsts, let him come to me and drink.
Whoever believes in me, as the Scripture has said,
Out of his heart will flow rivers of living water."

John 7:37-38 (ESV)

Our real thirst is quenched when we come open to the Lord to drink of Him. There's an old saying, "You can lead a horse to water, but you can't make it drink." Will you drink deeply of His river of delights today and experience the refreshing and abundant provisions He has in store for you? The hymn *I Heard the Voice of Jesus Say* encapsulates it well in its second stanza:

"Behold, I freely give
The living water: thirsty one,
Stoop down, and drink, and live."
I came to Jesus, and I drank
Of that life-giving stream;
My thirst was quenched, my soul revived,
And now I live in Him.

22

Dendrochronology

They went to a place called Gethsemane...

Mark 14:32 (NIV)

*D*endrochronology is the study of data from the growth of tree rings. Most people who enter into studying tree rings typically come from one of several disciplines: archaeology (for the purpose of dating materials and artefacts made from wood); chemists (tree rings are the method by which radiocarbon dates are calibrated); and scientists from the field of paleoclimatology where we can learn about the environmental conditions of the past, locally or globally, based on what the tree rings are telling us.

I came across an article, 'The Age of Olive Trees in the Garden of Gethsemane'. In this study a group of Italian scientists looked at eight olive trees in the Garden of Gethsemane, which is located in Jerusalem. They were radiocarbon-dated with a view to providing an estimate of their ages. Only three from a total of eight olive trees could be successfully dated. They were of the same age, having started life all through the 12th century. But the most intriguing discovery to have emerged from the analysis is that the eight olive trees are 'siblings' exhibiting an identical genetic profile, indicating that they belonged to the same 'mother' tree, a tree believed to have 'witnessed' the night of Jesus' agony.

The Garden of Gethsemane (Gethsemane means 'olive press') is an important location for us as it is the place where Jesus Christ prayed before He was crucified. Gethsemane was, and is, a place where olive trees grew and produced their fruit. The olives were collected, placed in a press and the precious olive oil was extracted from the olives under intense pressure. As the Synoptic Gospels recount, it was there that Jesus experienced his deepest anguish and experienced extreme pressure. At the edge of the Garden, Jesus left eight of the disciples, saying to them, "Sit ye here, while I shall pray."[12] He then took Peter, James and John with Him deeper into the Garden where He "began to be sore amazed, and to be very heavy; And saith unto them, My soul is exceeding sorrowful unto death: tarry ye here, and watch."[13] Never before have we seen Jesus so distraught. He had faced a raging storm on the Sea of Galilee totally composed and unruffled. He had emerged from the grilling of Jerusalem's religious leaders with total composure. But here in the Garden, Jesus cast Himself to the ground in agony. As Paul put it:

He humbled himself, and became obedient unto death, even the death of the cross.

Philippians 2:8 (KJV)

The passion Jesus displayed here has been depicted in musical works and films for centuries. From the 16th century, when Bach wrote two magnificent oratorios based on the Gospel accounts of Matthew and John, to the present day with the film *The Passion of the Christ*, the story of this extraordinary place has been told again and again. The most important impact of this 'olive press' occasion was the willingness of our Saviour to die on the cross in our place in order to pay the penalty for our sins. God "made Him who knew no sin to be sin for us, that we might become the righteousness of God in Him"[14]. It is at Gethsemane that we get a glimpse of just how much Jesus suffered in order to be our Saviour. It is, indeed, amazing love which caused the Son of God to voluntarily pursue the path of pain which led to the cross. Let's be thankful that He "went to a place called Gethsemane".

---

[12] Mark 14:32 (KJV)
[13] Mark 14:33-34 (KJV)
[14] 2 Corinthians 5:21 (NKJV)

23

Many Infallible Proofs

To whom also He showed himself alive after His passion by many infallible proofs, being seen of them forty days, and speaking of the things pertaining to the kingdom of God.

Acts 1:3 (NKJV)

*T*he Bible says that Jesus "showed himself alive after His passion by many infallible proofs". "Infallible proofs" is the translation of one Greek word *tekmerios*. It literally means 'indubitable evidence'. The New American Standard version puts it "convincing proofs" and the Amplified Bible says "convincing demonstrations".

Luke adds that there were "many" of them. The grave clothes, the empty tomb, Christ appearing alive to numerous people, the radical transformation of the disciples, were but a few. The disciples were frightened, confused, dazed, disoriented and disheartened. Every one of them was running for cover and they huddled in an upper room with the door locked for fear of the Jews. Fast forward a few weeks later. These same disciples now boldly stand in the temple courts preaching that Jesus Christ is Lord of all, that He has come back from the dead, and that only by repentance and faith can anyone be saved. What changed these cowering men and women from fear to faith, from doubters to believers, from cowards to martyrs, from dejected to joyous? There is only one credible explanation for such a radical change. They had seen the risen Christ and that sight had changed them forever. All but one died a martyr's death because of their testimony.

Paul says:

For I delivered to you first of all that which I also received: that Christ died for our sins according to the Scriptures, and that He was buried, and that He rose again the third day according to the Scriptures, and that He was seen by Cephas, then by the twelve. After that He was seen by over five hundred brethren at once, of whom the greater part remain to the present, but some have fallen asleep. After that He was seen by James, then by all the apostles. Then last of all He was seen by me also...

1 Corinthians 15:3-8 (NKJV)

Just as Jesus Christ transformed the lives of His disciples, so the lives of men and women throughout the years have also been transformed. On the Isle of Capri in the Bay of Naples, Italy, a local church has a traditional celebration every Easter Sunday. Each family brings with them a bird in a cage. Every Resurrection Sunday, the crowded church and the plaza outside are jammed with the people of Capri carrying cages. After the benediction, all of the cages are opened and the birds are released, to the joyous shout, "Christ has risen!" What freedom comes into our lives when we welcome the truth of the Resurrection.

24

Why Are You Weeping?

Jesus said to her, "Woman, why are you weeping? Whom are you seeking?"

John 20:15a (NKJV)

These were the first words Jesus spoke after His resurrection. They were spoken to Mary Magdalene. She was standing alone at the garden tomb about 6:30 a.m. on the first Easter Sunday. Her undying devotion had brought her to embalm the body of Jesus with spices. When she arrived, she found the stone rolled away and the tomb empty. She was devastated or, as we would say in Northern Ireland, 'gutted'. Horrifying loss, aching grief, powerlessness and emptiness would define her situation. In the darkness of her sorrow, Mary Magdalene needed someone to assure her that one day life would make sense again.

Mary was deeply upset by the shock of the crucifixion and now by the fact that tomb was empty. Why does Mary weep? She says:

"They have taken away my Lord and I do not know where they have laid him."

John 20:13 (ESV)

She must have been thinking, "If only I knew where they laid Him, I could finish embalming His body!" But she didn't understand the big picture, which included Jesus' resurrection.

Often, we too are like Mary. We're devastated because we don't understand the big picture of what God is doing. We're disappointed because God isn't working as we think He needs to work. We need to process our disappointments in light of the risen Saviour's love and care for us. We often don't understand His sovereign perspective. How hard it is to see clearly when devastating circumstances fill our eyes with tears. Everything gets blurry.

Notice Mary's ironic complaint, "They have taken away my Lord..."
It's ironic because He is right there with her! We have God's promise in
Hebrews 13:5...

He Himself has said, "I will never leave you nor forsake you."
Hebrews 13:5 (NKJV)

...yet we fail to see Him in our circumstances time and time again.
He is the risen Saviour and He is always involved in what involves you.
Paul said:

You do not grieve like the rest of mankind, who have no hope.
1 Thessalonians 4:13 (NIV)

Of course we grieve when we lose a loved one. But the Bible says that
although we grieve, we do not grieve as those who have no hope. The
hope that Jesus is risen, and that He is coming again to take us to be with
Him and with our loved ones who have died in Him, comforts us through
our tears.

Jesus does not gloss over our tears. "Why are you weeping?" Jesus
asks us. He immediately follows it with another question in verse 15:
"Whom are you seeking?"

What will our reply be? Will we be able to say honestly, "Lord, it is
You that I'm seeking in the midst of my trials."

Mary's weeping ceased in the presence of the resurrected Christ.
Mary had "seen the Lord" and her life was never the same again. May
we know that He is with us and He will never leave us nor forsake us.
May we experience what it means to be embraced by a God who knows
us intimately and, in spite of who we are, loves us enough to go to the
Cross.

25

He Saw and Believed

So Peter and the other disciple went forth, and they were going to the tomb. The two were running together; and the other disciple ran ahead faster than Peter and came to the tomb first; and stooping and looking in, he saw the linen wrappings lying there; but he did not go in. And so Simon Peter also came, following him, and entered the tomb; and he saw the linen wrappings lying there, and the face-cloth which had been on His head, not lying with the linen wrappings, but rolled up in a place by itself. So the other disciple who had first come to the tomb then also entered, and he saw and believed.

John 20:3-8 (NASB)

You may have noticed the repetition of the word "saw" in today's reading. What you would not know, unless you looked at the Greek text, is that John utilised three different Greek words for "saw".

Firstly, we are told that John "saw the linen wrappings lying there; but he did not go in". The Greek word translated "saw" in this verse is *bleep* which refers to a quick glance or a simple look. It was a mere viewing of the facts.

The second Greek word translated "saw" is in verse 6. Peter "saw the linen wrappings lying there, and the face-cloth which had been on His head, not lying with the linen wrappings, but rolled up in a place by itself". This Greek word for "saw" is *theoreo*, which carries the idea of 'looking carefully; to observe intensely or scrutinise'. We get our word 'theatre' from it. Peter's seeing was deeper because he went into the tomb and clearly saw something astounding. However, he did not yet understand completely.

The third "saw" is in verse 8 where we are told that John entered the tomb "and he saw and believed". This is the Greek word *eido* which means 'to perceive or look with understanding'. John perceived what had actually taken place. John's reaction from 'seeing' was 'believing'.

Peter had sight; John had insight. How about us this Easter? What do we see? Are we just peering into the pages of the Easter narrative and observing what happened? Or, are we perceiving and understanding that Jesus went to the Cross for us and when He cried out, "It is finished!"[15] it was not a terrified cry of defeat, but a triumphant cry of victory? It meant 'mission accomplished'. Are we perceiving the Bible's glorious message that He has risen[16] and is alive today?

> ...if you confess with your mouth Jesus as Lord, and believe in your heart that God raised Him from the dead, you will be saved.
>
> Romans 10:9 (NASB)

We need to be careful when we present the gospel that we remember the best part of the story. Not only did Jesus die for our sins on the cross, but He was raised from the dead. May the eyes of your heart may be enlightened[17] to this truth and may this truth transform our lives. May we 'see and believe'.

---

[15] John 19:30 (NKJV)
[16] See Matthew 28:6
[17] See Ephesians 1:18

26

The Silence of the Lamb

Then the high priest stood up before them and asked Jesus, 'Are you not going to answer? What is this testimony that these men are bringing against you?' But Jesus remained silent and gave no answer.

Mark 14:60-61 (NIVUK)

*T*he proverb says, "Speech is silver, but silence is golden." Jesus spoke very little throughout the timeline of trials leading up to his crucifixion. The vast majority of the accusations, questions, and lies of his persecutors were met by Jesus' silence. One of the clearest examples of Jesus staying silent was when he was before Herod.

When Herod saw Jesus, he was very glad, for he had long desired to see him, because he had heard about him, and he was hoping to see some sign done by him. So he questioned him at some length, but he made no answer.

Luke 23:8-9 (ESV)

Before the high priest we are told:

Then the high priest stood up before them and asked Jesus, 'Are you not going to answer? What is this testimony that these men are bringing against you?' But Jesus remained silent and gave no answer.

Mark 14:60-61 (NIVUK)

During the trial before Pilate, Matthew tells us:

When he was accused by the chief priests and the elders, he gave no answer. Then Pilate asked him, "Don't you hear the testimony they are bringing against you?" But Jesus made no reply, not even to a single charge – to the great amazement of the governor."

Matthew 27:12-14 (NIV)

So again Pilate asked him, 'Aren't you going to answer? See how many things they are accusing you of.' But Jesus still made no reply, and Pilate was amazed.

Mark 15:4-5 (NIVUK)

Over and over again the Bible records the silence of God's Lamb in the presence of His accusers. This is amazing, especially since the witnesses that were hurling charges against Jesus were giving false testimony. There is much He could have said in His defence. He could have undressed their arguments and addressed His situation with righteous rhetoric. Yet the same Lord of whom it was earlier said, "No one has ever spoken like this man," remained silent. Oswald Sanders writes in the book, *The Incomparable Christ:*

Both by His silence and His words, Jesus made clear that it was Pilate and the Jews who were on trial before Him, and not He before them.

He had at heart God's greater plan.
Peter stated:

When He was reviled, He did not revile in return; when He suffered, He did not threaten, but [here's the reason] continued entrusting Himself to Him who judges justly.

1 Peter 2:23 (ESV)

By not lashing out against His accusers, Jesus was saying, *my life is not in your hands, my life is in God's hands. It's all about His plan.* The prophet Isaiah had written of Him many years before:

He was oppressed and He was afflicted,
Yet He opened not His mouth;
He was led as a lamb to the slaughter,
And as a sheep before its shearers is silent,
So He opened not His mouth.

Isaiah 53:7 (NKJV)

It was necessary that He suffer and die for our redemption.
Let's appreciate not only His speech but His silence.

27

What is Written is Written

Now Pilate wrote a title and put it on the cross. And the writing was: JESUS OF NAZARETH, THE KING OF THE JEWS. Then many of the Jews read this title, for the place where Jesus was crucified was near the city; and it was written in Hebrew, Greek, and Latin. Therefore the chief priests of the Jews said to Pilate, "Do not write, 'The King of the Jews,' but, 'He said, "I am the King of the Jews."'" Pilate answered, "What I have written, I have written."

John 19:19-22 (NKJV)

*W*hy did Pilate post that sign? It was a custom by the Romans to hang what was called a *titulus* around a criminal's neck or have it carried before him on the way from the court to the place of execution. A *titulus* was a wooden tablet covered with gypsum and on it in black letters was written the charge by which the prisoner was condemned. It was affixed to the upper portion of the cross, above the criminal's head for all to see, and acted as a warning to obey the Roman law or face the consequences.

While it was customary for the condemned person to wear a placard giving his name and the nature of his crime, this sign, the sign on the Cross, was written in three languages – Hebrew, Greek, and Latin. It testified in three languages. In this fashion, the Romans would read it in their native tongue of Latin, the Jews would read it in Hebrew, and anyone else could read it in the common language of that day which was Greek. It was a sign for all the world to see. It was a witness to Jew and Gentile. It was a witness to residents of Israel, officials of Rome, and merchants and pilgrims from all over the Empire. The cross of Christ became a giant gospel tract for all who were passing by.

The Latin version mentioned in John, *IESUS NAZARENUS REX IOUDAEORM*, gives us the acronym INRI, an abbreviation which is found over the cross in so many images and early paintings of the crucifixion. The Early Church adopted as a symbol the Latin letters INRI. The importance of this is that Jesus is pictured as a universal Saviour. That does not mean that He will automatically save everybody, but that He will save anyone who will come to Him by faith regardless of their social standing or background. He is the Saviour of 'whosoever will'.[18]

What upset the chief priests? It is a point of Greek grammar! In English, there is a difference between saying 'the book' and 'a book'. 'The' is called the definite article, and it indicates one particular, definite book; whereas 'a' is the indefinite article, and it indicates any book, not yet specified. In Greek, there is also a definite article and it is used in Pilate's inscription, referring to *The* King of the Jews, an absolute title. They said to Pilate, "Do not write, 'The King of the Jews.'" But Pilate said, "What I have written, I have written." Jesus is the One and Only King of kings. The title on the Cross is forever true, and in Revelation 19:16 Jesus is given the full title, "King of kings and Lord of lords"[19]. May the message of the Cross be understandable to us all and may we bow our knees to the Name above all names.

---

[18] See John 3:16; Revelation 22:17
[19] ESV

28

A Reservoir of Tears

Oh, that my head were waters and my eyes a reservoir of tears,
that I might weep day and night for the slain of the daughter
of my people!

Jeremiah 9:1 (AMPC)

hemists tell us that tears are a combination of sodium chloride, phosphate of lime, mucus and water. Medics will confirm that tears are secretions that clean and lubricate the eyes. Lacrimation is apparently the technical term for the production or shedding of tears.

Jeremiah was known as the weeping prophet. He wrote Lamentations in addition to the book of Jeremiah and we can see how his heart is broken for his people.

My eyes fail from weeping, I am in torment within; my heart
is poured out on the ground because my people are destroyed,
because children and infants faint in the streets of the city.

Lamentations 2:11 (NIV)

Streams of tears flow from my eyes because my people are
destroyed. My eyes will flow unceasingly, without relief.

Lamentations 3:48-49 (NIV)

Likewise, Nehemiah was moved to tears.

When I heard these things, I sat down and wept. For some
days I mourned and fasted and prayed before the God of
heaven.

Nehemiah 1:4 (NIV)

Listen to the Psalmist too.

My tears have been my food day and night, while men say to
me all day long, "Where is your God?"

Psalm 42:3 (AMPC)

You have kept count of my tossings;
* put my tears in your bottle.*
Are they not in your book?

Psalm 56:8 (ESV)

Streams of tears flow from my eyes,
* for your law is not obeyed.*

Psalm 119:136 (NIV)

Jesus cried.

As he approached Jerusalem and saw the city, He wept over it.

Luke 19:41 (NIV)

During the days of Jesus' life on earth, He offered up prayers and petitions with loud cries and tears to the one who could save Him from death, and He was heard because of His reverent submission.

Hebrews 5:7 (NIV)

Paul cried. He said:

"I served the Lord with great humility and with tears, although I was severely tested by the plots of the Jews."

Acts 20:19 (NIV)

For I wrote you out of great distress and anguish of heart and with many tears, not to grieve you but to let you know the depth of my love for you.

2 Corinthians 2:4 (NIV)

For, as I have often told you before and now say again even with tears, many live as enemies of the cross of Christ.

Philippians 3:18 (NIV)

How about us?

Let us learn to think of tears as liquid prayers; and of weeping as a constant dropping of importunate intercession which will wear its way right surely into the very heart of mercy, despite the stony difficulties which obstruct the way.

Charles H. Spurgeon (1834-1892)

29

Let the Redeemed of the Lord Say So

Oh give thanks to the LORD, for He is good,
For His lovingkindness is everlasting.
Let the redeemed of the LORD say so,
Whom He has redeemed from the hand of the adversary.

Psalm 107:1-2 (NASB)

*W*e are called "the redeemed of the Lord". When we look at our English word "redeemed", the first three letters say it all: *red*. Red reminds us of the precious blood shed for our redemption. There are a number of different words used in the original Greek which are translated into English as "redeemed", each giving us another nuance of its meaning.

The first is *agorazo*. The noun *agora* is Greek for a 'marketplace', a wide, open public space. The English word 'agoraphobia' is derived from it, meaning a fear of open spaces. The verb *agorazo* translated as "redeemed" literally means 'to do business in the marketplace', in other words, to buy, to purchase or to acquire ownership by payment of a price. We know the purchase price in our case is the blood of God's own Son.

For ye are bought with a price.

1 Corinthians 6:20 (KJV)

...you were not redeemed with corruptible things, like silver or gold, from your aimless conduct received by tradition from your fathers, but with the precious blood of Christ, as of a lamb without blemish and without spot. He indeed was foreordained before the foundation of the world, but was manifest in these last times for you.

1 Peter 1:18-20 (NKJV)

The second is *exagorazo*. Look familiar? It is the same word as above with *ex* on the front of it. That means it is a strengthened form of *agorazo*. *Ex* means 'out of' – think of exit, way out. We have been redeemed out of something, into something. Paul said;

> *Who hath delivered us from the power of darkness, and hath translated us into the kingdom of his dear Son: in whom we have redemption through his blood, even the forgiveness of sins.*
>
> *Colossians 1:13 (KJV)*

The third word is *lutroo*. The root of *lutroo*, *luo*, means 'to loosen, unbind or untie, to set at liberty'. It was the price of release, the substitution of money for a slave in order to set him free. The underlying purpose behind Christ's redemptive work is freedom to fulfil our potential.

> *Who gave Himself for us, that He might redeem us from all iniquity, and purify unto Himself a peculiar people, zealous of good works.*
>
> *Titus 2:14 (KJV)*

Let's "give thanks to the Lord, for He is good, for His lovingkindness is everlasting. Let the redeemed of the Lord say so, whom He has redeemed from the hand of the adversary."

30

The Curriculum of Contentment

Not that I speak in respect of want: for I have learned, in whatsoever state I am, therewith to be content. I know both how to be abased, and I know how to abound: everywhere and in all things I am instructed both to be full and to be hungry, both to abound and to suffer need. I can do all things through Christ which strengtheneth me.

Philippians 4:11-13 (KJV)

Much of the business world works hard to breed discontent so that we will buy products and keep the economy vibrant. If an advertisement tells us that something is new and improved, we are supposed to feel that we have less than the best and must go out and buy the next thing.

The poem captures the idea:

It was spring, but it was summer I wanted;
  the warm days and the great outdoors.
It was summer, but it was fall I wanted;
  the colourful leaves and the cool dry air.
It was fall, but it was winter I wanted;
  the beautiful snow and the joy of the holiday season.
It was winter, but it was spring that I wanted;
  the warmth and the blossoming of nature.
I was a child, but it was adulthood I wanted;
  the freedom and the respect.
I was 20, but it was 30 I wanted;
  to be mature and sophisticated.
I was middle-aged, but it was 20 I wanted;
  the youth and the free spirit.
I was retired, but it was middle-age I wanted;
  the presence of mind without limitation.

My life was over;
but I never got what I wanted.

All the world lives in two tents – content and discontent. You will notice in this passage that Paul says, "…I have learned to be content…"[20] The word "content" is a very interesting one. It comes from a Greek word *autarkes* which means 'to have all needed within'. It means 'independent of external circumstances'. It was used to describe a city or country that needed no imports. They had all they needed to sustain life. It is a vivid picture of the believer who has Christ dwelling within. He is the All-Sufficient Saviour. All joy, all peace, all wisdom, all meaning, value, purpose, hope, fulfilment in life now and forever is bound up in Christ. Warren Wiersbe states:

The word "content" actually means "contained." It is a description of the man whose resources are within him so that he does not have to depend on substitutes without.

Paul expresses it in his own words in verse 13:

I can do all things through Christ which strengtheneth me.
Philippians 4:13 (KJV)

Charles Wesley expressed it in this way:

Thou, O Christ, art all I want,
More than all in Thee I find.

Is discontentment your default setting or have you learned to be content?

---

[20]   Philippian 4:11 (AMP)

31

Come and Worship

...where morning dawns, where evening fades,
you call forth songs of joy.

Psalm 65:8 (NIV)

From where the sun rises to where it sets,
* you inspire shouts of joy.*

Psalm 65:8 (NLT)

Dawn and dusk take turns calling, "Come and worship."

Psalm 65:8 (MSG)

Which is your favourite — a beautiful sunrise or a beautiful sunset? That's a hard choice, isn't it? Take a moment to go back and read the opening verses again, slowly, with reverence.

Our rising hours are bright with hope, and our evening moments mellow with thanksgiving. Notice that our response to every sunrise and every sunset is joyful worship. We wake up with praise; we wind down with praise.

Praise the Lord! (Hallelujah!) Praise, O servants of the Lord,
praise the name of the Lord! Blessed be the name of the Lord
from this time forth and forever. From the rising of the sun to
the going down of it and from east to west, the name of the
Lord is to be praised!

Psalm 113:1-3 (AMPC)

From east to west, from dawn to dusk, keep lifting all your praises to God! Or, as the Living Bible states:

Praise Him from sunrise to sunset!

Psalm 113:3 (TLB)

No matter where you are in the world, no matter what time of day it is, every moment of every day God inspires shouts of joy. His Name is to be praised. We should be always wearing the garment of praise.[21]

God says:

> For from the rising of the sun even to its setting,
> My name will be great among the nations.
>
> *Malachi 1:11 (NASB)*

John Calvin rightly said:

> There is not a corner in heaven or on earth where God is not praised.

Psalm 92 tells us:

> It is good to give thanks to the LORD
>   and to sing praises to Your name, O Most High;
> to declare Your lovingkindness in the morning
>   and Your faithfulness by night.
>
> *Psalm 92:1-2 (NASB)*

He says, it is good!

> Praise the LORD!
> For it is good to sing praises to our God;
>   for it is pleasant and praise is becoming.
>
> *Psalm 147:1 (ESV)*

It is good to praise.
Remember:

> This is the day that the LORD has made,
>   let us rejoice and be glad in it.
>
> *Psalm 118:24 (ESV)*

---

[21] See Isaiah 61:3

March

April

April

1

Bluebell Season

But let all who take refuge in you be glad; let them ever sing for joy. Spread your protection over them, that those who love your name may rejoice in you.

Psalm 5:11 (NIV)

Portglenone Forest Park, approximately half a mile from where I live, is beautiful and relaxing at any time of year. However, in April and May it becomes a magnet for visitors from all across the country due to the bluebell season. Carpets of intense blue cover the grounds with swathes of swaying colour and diffuse a sweet scent into the air attracting the attention of plenty of pollinating insects.

I was surprised to learn that almost half the world's iconic bluebells are found in the UK and are relatively rare in the rest of the world. We know the familiar bulbous bluebell under various names such as wild hyacinth, wood bell, bell bottle, Cuckoo's Boots, Wood Hyacinth and Lady's Nightcap. It was Swedish botanist Carl Linnaeus who formalised the bluebell's binomial nomenclature as *Hyacinthoides non-scripta* which basically means an 'unmarked' hyacinth.

In the United Kingdom, the British Bluebell is a protected species under the Wildlife and Countryside Act 1981. It is a criminal offence to uproot the wild common bluebell from land on which it naturally grows. Any trade in wild common bluebell bulbs or seeds is also an offence, carrying fines of up to £5,000 per bulb. Bluebells are protected because they face many threats and are an important species to preserve. Threats include the loss of ancient woodland habitat, the illegal collection of bulbs and hybridisation with non-native bluebells.

As I considered the bluebell this week, I was reminded of how God spreads His protection over us. The Hebrew word for "spread your protection" in today's passage means 'to cover, defend, hedge in, put a fence around'. It is translated as "covering" in Exodus 25:20:

April

> *And the cherubim shall stretch out their wings above, covering the mercy seat with their wings...*
>
> *Exodus 25:20 (NKJV)*

In Psalm 91 David stated:

> *He will cover you with his feathers,*
>   *and under his wings you will find refuge...*
>
> *Psalm 91:4 (NIV)*

Again, he verified:

> *You are my hiding place;*
>   *you will protect me from trouble*
>   *and surround me with songs of deliverance.*
>
> *Psalm 32:7 (NIV)*

Remember that you are much more than an 'unmarked' hyacinth.

> *When you believed, you were marked in Him with a seal, the promised Holy Spirit.*
>
> *Ephesians 1:13 (NIV)*

Yes, you have been marked with His seal of ownership. May He spread His protection over you today.

2

In the Departure Lounge

For I am now ready to be offered, and the time of my departure is at hand. I have fought a good fight, I have finished my course, I have kept the faith.

2 Timothy 4:6-7 (KJV)

These are Paul's 'exit lines' before his martyrdom in A.D. 67. On his deathbed, Napoleon said:

I die before my time and my body will be given back to earth to become the food of worms such is the fate which so soon awaits the great Napoleon.

Charles Darwin said:

I was a young man with unformed ideas. I threw out queries, suggestions, wondering all the time about everything. To my astonishment the ideas took like wild-fire. People made a religion of them.

Sir Michael Faraday (English scientist 1791-1867) said:

I rest upon Jesus Christ who died, and rose again from death.

Paul says, "I am now ready" – powerful, confident words! He was ready because he had trusted Christ as his Saviour.

...I know whom I have believed...

2 Timothy 1:12 (NKJV)

"The time of my departure is at hand." The Greek word for "departure" means 'loosening the ropes of a tent' and refers to temporary pilgrims on this earth awaiting a permanent home in heaven. Paul looks back over thirty years of ministry and describes in three brief expressions in verse 7, "I have fought a good fight, I have finished my course, I have kept the faith." Paul had no regret, no sense of unfulfillment or incompleteness since he has given Christ control of his life.

- "I have fought the good fight."
- "I have finished my course."
- "I have kept the faith."

He was a fighter! He was a finisher! He was faithful! May we be able to say the same.

3

Empty Vessels

So Elisha said to her, "What shall I do for you? Tell me, what do you have in the house?" And she said, "Your maidservant has nothing in the house but a jar of oil." Then he said, "Go, borrow vessels from everywhere, from all your neighbours – empty vessels; do not gather just a few. And when you have come in, you shall shut the door behind you and your sons; then pour it into all those vessels, and set aside the full ones." So she went from him and shut the door behind her and her sons, who brought the vessels to her; and she poured it out. Now it came to pass, when the vessels were full, that she said to her son, "Bring me another vessel." And he said to her, "There is not another vessel." So the oil ceased.

2 Kings 4:2-6 (NKJV)

his is the story of Elisha and the widow's oil. To the logical but unbelieving mind, it would appear foolish to gather a lot of empty vessels to hold oil when you did not know where the oil was coming from! What was she going to do with empty jars? She was already empty and yet she was told to go and gather some more emptiness. No matter how strange or unusual or illogical it may seem, when God says it, we must do it.

God is looking for empty vessels today. We are referred to as earthen vessels in the Bible.

But we have this treasure in earthen vessels, that the excellence of the power may be of God and not of us.

2 Corinthians 4:7 (NKJV)

When we empty ourselves of self-righteousness and pride and the cares of this world, God can fill us with the power of His Holy Spirit (symbolised by oil) and we can pour out our lives as a blessing to others.

Notice that the number of vessels to be brought was "not ... just a few". In other words, bring as many as you have faith that God will fill. The number of empty vessels brought into the house showed the woman's faith, obedience and her submission to God. The size of her blessing was directly related to how obedient she had been in getting the jars. God's ability to provide always exceeds our capacity to receive. The oil flowed until the vessels ran out. When the day was done, every vessel was filled to the full. There was no limit on the amount of oil. The only limit was on the amount of vessels. God's provision knew no limits in the widow's case and it knows no limits in our case! God is able to meet every need, move every mountain and solve every problem. God's sufficiency is more than enough for every deficiency in our lives.

God is looking for empty vessels to fill. He is looking for people who have died to self and desire to be filled with His Spirit. He is looking for people who will take Him at His word and not limit Him.

May we be channels of blessing to those around us today.

4

Last but Not Least: Self-Control

Like a city whose walls are broken down is a man who lacks self-control.

Proverbs 25:28 (NIV)

A person without self-control is like a city with broken-down walls. When the book of Proverbs was written, one of the main sources of strength and protection for a city consisted in the building and maintaining of walls. A wiped-out wall was considered a breach in security. A city with walls in disrepair was a city with a shameful reputation. That's one of the reasons why Nehemiah was so motivated to begin a building campaign in Nehemiah 1:3. Those who lived in the capital were in "great trouble and disgrace"[22] because the wall of Jerusalem was broken down. It was open to attack and ultimate destruction. The man or woman who lacks self-restraint is like a city that has no effective defence. The enemy can walk in and out with ease.

So the most important feature of a city in biblical times was its walls. And a no less important part of our character has to be self-control. A person who lacks self-control is defenceless, open to defeat and destruction by the enemy.

In Galatians 5 Paul listed the fruit of the Spirit:

But the Holy Spirit produces this kind of fruit in our lives: love, joy, peace, patience, kindness, goodness, faithfulness, gentleness, and self-control.

Galatians 5:22-23 (NLT)

These are not listed in order of importance. Self-control is last but certainly not least. It is of extreme importance and sadly will be lacking in the last days.[23] While "self-control" is a good translation of the Greek

---

[22] Nehemiah 1:3 (NIV)
[23] Read 2 Timothy 3

word, it's a bit deceiving because we all know that we can't control ourselves simply through our own willpower or self-determination. The Greek word literally mean 'power from within' and reminds us that it is the work of the Holy Spirit within us that accomplishes this.

The Bible tells us that we can say no to ungodliness and live self-controlled lives.

> *For the grace of God has appeared that offers salvation to all people. It teaches us to say "No" to ungodliness and worldly passions, and to live self-controlled, upright and godly lives in this present age.*
>
> *Titus 2:11-12 (NIV)*

Challenge for today: are you keeping in step with the Spirit or is your life out-of-control? Remember, when you forfeit the fruit of self-control, you are feeble and open to attack.

5

Digging Ditches

And he said, "Thus says the LORD: 'Make this valley full of ditches.' For thus says the LORD: 'You shall not see wind, nor shall you see rain; yet that valley shall be filled with water, so that you, your cattle, and your animals may drink.' And this is a simple matter in the sight of the Lord..."

2 Kings 3:16-18 (NKJV)

*H*ere we see the importance of digging ditches. Basically, the Lord is saying, "Prepare for a flood in the desert." Elisha directs the kings and their armies to dig ditches in the desert valley. They are to fill the valley with ditches, or trenches, for the Lord is going to provide water.

This is not the first time the Lord requires His people do something seemingly illogical:

- The Lord tells Noah to build a large ark and gather the animals for the coming worldwide flood.
- The Lord tells Abraham to take Isaac, through whom are the covenant promises of God, upon the mount and sacrifice him.
- At the Lord's command Joshua instructs Israel to march around Jericho once a day for six days and then seven times on the seventh day. At the end of the seventh round the people were to shout and the walls would fall down.

When these commands are obeyed, then the promises of God are fulfilled. These commands always require faith on man's part and a miracle on God's part.

In their thirst and utter exhaustion, they set about digging ditches, but there is no immediate result. They are in the desert in the tormenting heat and full of thirst, and they are just digging. However, after their long day of digging, they retire to bed and the next morning they wake up and find that water has filled the land. Only God can send the rain. God asked them to do the possible and He did the impossible. We know with God nothing is impossible. In fact, it says in verse 18, "...this is a simple matter in the sight of the Lord."

In 1867, C.H. Spurgeon said:

> *Be prepared to receive that which He is about to give; each man in his place and each woman in her sphere, make the whole of this Church full of trenches for the reception of the Divine Floods.*

6

Have You Discovered Your Spiritual Eyes?

And when the servant of the man of God arose early and went out, there was an army, surrounding the city with horses and chariots. And his servant said to him, "Alas, my master! What shall we do?" So he answered, "Do not fear, for those who are with us are more than those who are with them."And Elisha prayed, and said, "LORD, I pray, open his eyes that he may see." Then the LORD opened the eyes of the young man, and he saw. And behold, the mountain was full of horses and chariots of fire all around Elisha.

2 Kings 6:15-17 (NKJV)

Notice Elisha's prayer: "...open his eyes so he may see." He wasn't literally blind because he saw the Syrians. He was simply unable to perceive spiritual reality. He could see the danger, but not the deliverance!

Jesus quoted from Jeremiah to chide his disciples for their lack of spiritual awareness:

"You have eyes but you do not see."

Jeremiah 5:21 (NIV)

The Four-Eyed Fish, a minnow-like fish, makes its home in Central and South America. The unusual feature about this fish is its large, bulging eyes. It has eyes raised above the top of its head and divided in two different parts, bifocals, so that it can see below and above the water surface at the same time. This is the kind of discerning vision we should have as Christians. We need to have our eyes fixed on the needs of those around us and be aware of the snares of the enemy; but at the same time, we should be tuned in above to the power that's available for us, to the protection that surrounds us, to the provision that's there for us. As a follower of Jesus Christ, we are under constant raid by the enemy, but don't forget we are also under the constant radar of God.

Paul says:

> *I pray that the eyes of your heart may be enlightened, so that you will know what is the hope of His calling, what are the riches of the glory of His inheritance in the saints, and what is the surpassing greatness of His power toward us who believe.*
>
> *Ephesians 1:18-19 (NASB)*

Have you discovered your spiritual eyes? Are you seeing your circumstances through the eyes of faith? Are you saying, "Alas what shall we do?" or are you declaring, "Those who are with us are more than those who are with them"?

7

Shake It Off

But when Paul had gathered a bundle of sticks and laid them on the fire, a viper came out because of the heat and fastened itself on his hand. When the natives saw the creature hanging from his hand, they began saying to one another, "Undoubtedly this man is a murderer, and though he has been saved from the sea, justice has not allowed him to live." However he shook the creature off into the fire and suffered no harm.

Acts 28:3-5 (NASB)

The Apostle Paul and 275 others were sailing across the Mediterranean Sea, Paul on his way to stand trial before Caesar in Rome, when they encountered a horrific storm which caused the ship to strike a sandbar and break up off an island called Malta. The crew jumped off the ship, some swimming to shore and others grabbing hold of pieces of the ship, drifting to the island. They all arrived safely as God had promised!

The islanders showed extraordinary kindness by lighting a fire to warm the crew. Paul was helping gather wood for the fire. As he laid his bundle of sticks in the flames, a poisonous snake came out and bit him, hanging onto his hand. Paul shook the snake off and the people waited to see what would happen to him. In verse 5 we see how Paul responded:

But Paul shook the snake off into the fire and suffered no ill effects.

Acts 28:5 (NIV)

Has the devil come out of the woodwork and attacked you in some way? Is he trying to inject his poisonous venom into your life? Through the power of God, you can also shake off the challenges that are thrown at you. Rise up, shake off the snake and walk in the light of who you are in Christ.

8

Smite Your Eyes

But you shall utterly exterminate them, the Hittites, the Amorites, the Canaanites, the Perizzites, the Hivites, and the Jebusites, as the Lord your God has commanded you.

Deuteronomy 20:17 (AMPC)

*W*hat are your 'ites'? The nations ending in 'ite,' such as Hittite, have special meanings and represent what the enemy tries to throw at us today to deflect us from our spiritual walk. For example, Hittite means 'sons of terror, fear and insecurity'. It's time to conquer the 'ites' in our lives and completely destroy them so that we can pursue God's purposes. Leave no room or foothold for the enemy to work.

Do you remember in 1 Samuel 15:3 the Lord commissioned Saul to utterly destroy all of the Amalekites? It was a clear, radical command.

"Now go, attack the Amalekites and totally destroy everything that belongs to them. Do not spare them."

1 Samuel 15:3 (NIV)

Instead, what did Saul do? On the surface he obeyed but it was a selective, incomplete obedience. Saul was determined to listen to the opinions of others and not God.

Saul and the troops spared Agag, and the best of the sheep, cattle, and choice animals, as well as the young rams and the best of everything else. They were not willing to destroy them, but they did destroy all the worthless and unwanted things.

1 Samuel 15:9 (HCSB)

Sadly for Saul, partial obedience is disobedience. In 1 Samuel 30, the Amalekites showed up again! This time they attacked the Israelite settlement of Ziklag, burnt it to the ground and carried off everyone as prisoners. Saul's disobedience caused such heartache and grief for David and his men.

> *We cannot obey partially or halfheartedly as we seek to eliminate sin from our lives. We cannot stop while the task remains incomplete. Sins, like Amalekites, have a way of escaping the slaughter, breeding, reviving, regrouping, and launching new and unexpected assaults on our most vulnerable areas.*
>
> *John MacArthur*

Let us "totally destroy" every sin that hinders our walk with God.

9

Ready or Not, Here he Comes

He who testifies to these things says, "Yes, I am coming soon."
Amen. Come, Lord Jesus.

Revelation 22:20 (NIV)

One of the most memorable games from my childhood days is the game of hide and seek. When the game started, someone was chosen to be 'it'. A spot was chosen to be 'base'. Whoever was 'it' would stand at 'base', close their eyes and count to a hundred. The other players ran and hid. When the person who was 'it' finished counting, he or she would say, "Ready or not, here I come," and run to find everyone. I can remember playing the game and hearing 'it' say, "Ready or not, here I come," and getting rattled because I hadn't found the perfect hiding place and wasn't ready.

Jesus is coming! Sceptics and scoffers deny that fact, but they can't change the truth of it. Jesus Christ is coming again soon. He warns us to be ready for His coming. The countdown has begun and we need to realise that, *ready or not, here He comes!*

In Matthew 25 we can read the parable of the ten bridesmaids. Five of them were foolish, and five were wise. The wise ones were ready for the Bridegroom's return. Suddenly, the ten bridesmaids hear a shout:

'Look! Here is the bridegroom!'

Matthew 25:6 (NRSV)

The five wise bridesmaids have their lamps ready, but the five foolish bridesmaids don't have any oil to light their lamps. The five foolish ask the wise to borrow some oil, but the wise bridesmaids refuse because there isn't enough oil to share. The foolish ones are instructed to go and buy oil, and the bridegroom returns while they are gone. Jesus says:

"And while they went to buy it, the bridegroom came, and those who were ready went with him into the wedding banquet; and the door was shut. Later the other bridesmaids

came also, saying, 'Lord, lord, open to us.' But he replied, 'Truly I tell you, I do not know you.'"

Matthew 25:10-12 (NRSV)

Jesus then says:

"Watch therefore, for you know neither the day nor the hour in which the Son of Man is coming."

Matthew 25:13 (NKJV)

Are you ready or not?

10

Excuses

Moses answered God, "But why me? What makes you think that I could ever go to Pharaoh and lead the children of Israel out of Egypt?"

Exodus 3:11 (MSG)

*T*he Bible is littered with excuse-makers. Take for example Moses.

Excuse 1: "I'm not good enough."

"Who am I that I should go to Pharaoh, and that I should bring the children of Israel out of Egypt?"

Exodus 3:11 (NKJV)

Excuse 2: "I don't have all the answers."

Then Moses said to God, "Indeed, when I come to the children of Israel and say to them, 'The God of your fathers has sent me to you,' and they say to me, 'What is His name?' what shall I say to them?"

Exodus 3:13 (NKJV)

Excuse 3: "People won't believe me."

Then Moses answered and said, "But suppose they will not believe me or listen to my voice; suppose they say, 'The LORD has not appeared to you.'"

Exodus 4:1 (NKJV)

Excuse 4: "I'm a terrible public speaker."

Then Moses said to the LORD, "O my Lord, I am not eloquent, neither before nor since You have spoken to Your servant; but I am slow of speech and slow of tongue."

Exodus 4:10 (NKJV)

Excuse 5: "I'm not qualified."

But he said, "O my Lord, please send by the hand of whomever else You may send."

Exodus 4:13 (NKJV)

Do you recognise any of these excuses in yourself? Excuses in our lives give us permission to settle for less than God's best. It seems we always have an excuse or makeshift justification for why we cannot do something. You can do all things through Christ who gives you strength! He can give you supernatural qualifications. He can cause you to be at the right place at the right time. When God gives you something to do, He always gives you the enabling grace to do it, regardless of how dauntingly impossible the task may seem.

What have you been putting off in sheer avoidance or because of the enemy's voice whispering thoughts of failure, incompetence and lack of qualification? The Moses of Exodus chapters 3 and 4 is the same man that shows remarkable courage, obedience and strength of character a few chapters later. God works with each of us where we are and takes us to where He wants us to be. We just need to be willing to leave behind the excuses. Billy Sunday said:

An excuse is a skin of a reason stuffed with a lie.

11

Mountain to Molehill

This is the word of the LORD to Zerubbabel saying, 'Not by might nor by power, but by My Spirit,' says the LORD of hosts. 'What are you, O great mountain? Before Zerubbabel you will become a plain.'

Zechariah 4:6-7 (NASB)

$\mathcal{P}$eering through the Georgian window of my office, I have a clear vista of the Sperrins mountain range with its undulating hills, pocketed with valleys of bogland. Only a few miles away I can also physically step onto Slemish mountain, a popular tourist spot and heritage site because of its association with St. Patrick. It rises to a height of nearly 1,500 feet (450 metres) which is rather small in comparison to the mountain ranges of the world.

Zechariah 4:7 mentions a particular "mountain" which needed attention. In the Amplified Bible we read:

"For who are you, O great mountain [of human obstacles]? Before Zerubbabel [who with Joshua had led the return of the exiles from Babylon and was undertaking the rebuilding of the temple, before him] you shall become a plain [a mere molehill]!"

Zechariah 4:7 (AMPC)

The Message Bible states:

"So, big mountain, who do you think you are? Next to Zerubbabel you're nothing but a molehill."

Zechariah 4:7 (MSG)

In context, the Jews had returned to Judah after the Babylonian Exile and their temple needed to be rebuilt. The construction site had laid dormant for sixteen years. The rebuilding was at a standstill and the longer it loomed, the harder it probably seemed. The task before them seemed like a mountain to climb, it was all uphill and daunting, but God assured Zerubbabel that the "mountain" would become a plain by the Spirit of God. Zerubbabel received a promise from the Lord, that no mountain, no matter how great, could stop the purposes of God! He was encouraged not to look at things from a human and earthly point of view, but to trust the supernatural power of God to bring about what He had promised.

What are the different mountain ranges or overwhelming obstacles you face in your life? What is your particular mountain today? What is that mountain which seems big, looming, hard to overcome, difficult to see past or seemingly impossible to climb? How would you like all your mountains to become mere molehills or smooth terrain?

God says it is possible only "by My Spirit". It is not in our own might and power. God is more than capable of levelling the mountain of obstacles that are before you! Trust Him!

12

The Perfect Pattern

For you have been called for this purpose, since Christ also suffered for you, leaving you an example for you to follow in His steps...

1 Peter 2:21 (NASB)

I can remember back to kindergarten days when we were faced with the daunting task of learning how to write. Having been taught how to grip a pencil, we were given copy books with faint letters of the alphabet and our task was to trace over them and become familiar with their shape. Eventually, after many clumsy and arduous efforts, we learnt how to write our names and form basic words.

All of this experience flooded back into my mind as I studied the above verse found in 1 Peter 2. It tells us that Christ has left us "an example". The Greek word for "example" is *hupogrammos.* It is a school word related to Greek elementary education. It refers to the act of writing over letters. Teachers would lightly trace the letters of the alphabet so that students could write over them to learn how to write. Just as a child slowly, with laborious effort and close application, follows the shape of the letters of his teacher and thus learns the art of writing, so we should with similar effort, and by close application to our daily lives, endeavour to be like the Lord Jesus.

John phrased it this way:

Whoever claims to live in him must live as Jesus did.

1 John 2:6 (NIV)

Paul understood this and said:

Follow my example, as I follow the example of Christ.

1 Corinthians 11:1 (NIV)

In similar manner he told us:

You must have the same attitude that Christ Jesus had.

Philippians 2:5 (NLT)

Remember, the closer you are, the easier it is to follow. Jesus is our example. Walk closely with Christ each day and allow Him to reproduce His characteristics in your life.

Are you following the perfect pattern?

13

Pink Flamingos

Your words were found and I ate them, and Your words became for me a joy and the delight of my heart.

Jeremiah 15:16

*I*f you had asked me last week, "What does a flamingo look like?" I would have described its basic anatomy to you in this way: flamingos are large birds which are clearly identifiable by their long necks, sticklike legs, backward-bending knees and most noticeably they have pink feathers. That was my answer before I flicked through the channels one night and landed on a nature documentary about flamingos. Here the birds featured close-up were undeniably grey or white! They had the shape and silhouette of a typical flamingo, but they were not pink. What was going on? I listened attentively as the reporter informed us that flamingos are not pink. They are born with grey feathers which gradually turn pink because of their diet.

Apparently, everything about a flamingo is pink only because of its food. They are pink because the algae they consume is loaded with beta carotene, an organic chemical that contains a reddish-orange pigment. As zoos and attractions began to feature pink flamingos, they found that their colour would fade and their young were not quite as pink as those in the wild. By increasing the brine shrimp in their diet which is rich in carotenoids, they found the pink and orange hue returned to their feathers.

Flamingos embody the saying "you are what you eat". So, what are we feeding on spiritually? People who spend regular time in the Lord's presence with His Word are changed from the inside out literally. The more you devour the Word of God and feast on His precepts, the more vivid the change. The psalmist wrote:

Thy word have I hid in mine heart, that I might not sin against thee.

Psalm 119:11 (KJV)

He understood that what is on the inside effects what is on the outside. The Old Testament prophet Jeremiah said:

> *Your words were found and I ate them, and Your word became to me the gladness and joy of my heart.*
>
> *Jeremiah 15:16 (NIV)*

God's Word had a positive effect on his heart.

May we feed on God's Word and allow the transformation to be seen in our lives.

14

What Manner of Man is This?

But the men marvelled, saying, What manner of man is this,
that even the winds and the sea obey him!

Matthew 8:27 (KJV)

*J*esus had just circumvented the very laws of nature by calming a
storm. With one quick word, the storm abated and the sea became
calm. The disciples marvelled at this powerful display of Jesus'
supernatural ability over the elements and declared, "What manner of
man is this, that even the winds and the sea obey Him!"

What manner of man is this? It's a great question for us to ask, and a
careful consideration of the Gospels will rewardingly reveal to us His
person and purpose. There is no-one who can compare to Him!

- *No-one ever spoke like Him!*
  In John 7 when the officers who had been sent by the chief
  priests and Pharisees to take the Lord Jesus into custody
  returned without Him, they gave a most extraordinary reason
  for their failure to carry out their orders. For, in reply to the
  demand, "Why have ye not brought Him?"[24] they gave the
  strange answer, "Never man spake like this man."[25]

- *No name compares to His.*
  His is the Name above all names. Philippians 2:9 says,
  "Therefore God also has highly exalted Him and given Him the
  name which is above every name."

- *His peace is unparalleled.*
  According to Philippians 4:7, it "surpasses all understanding"[26]
  or as the Living Bible (TLB) states, "...it is far more wonderful
  than the human mind can understand."

---

[24] John 7:45 (KJV)
[25] John 7:46 (KJV)
[26] NKJV

- *His love is unlimited and has neither brim nor bottom.*
  Ephesians 3:18 talks about "how wide and long and high and deep is the love of Christ"[27].
- *His joy is inexpressible.*
  1 Peter 1:8 says, "You love Him even though you have never seen Him; though not seeing Him, you trust Him; and even now you are happy with the inexpressible joy that comes from heaven itself."[28]

The goal of Paul's life was to know Him more and more...

...that I may know Him (that I may progressively become more deeply and intimately acquainted with Him, perceiving and recognising and understanding the wonders of His Person more strongly and more clearly).

Philippians 3:10 (AMPC)

No wonder Paul concluded with the words:

Thanks be to God for His indescribable gift!

2 Corinthians 9:15 (AMP)

He is indescribable. He's the superlative of everything good.

---

[27] NIV
[28] TLB

15

A Precious Pearl

Consider it pure joy, my brothers, whenever you face trials of many kinds, because you know that the testing of your faith develops perseverance. Perseverance must finish its work so that you may be mature and complete, not lacking anything.

James 1:2-4 (NIV)

*I*t takes an oyster somewhere between three and six years to produce a perfect pearl. The process begins with a small piece of sand or other irritant entering the oyster. A pearl is a product of pain and suffering. A pearl is formed when an oyster gets a grain of sand trapped in the soft flesh inside its shell. This piece of sand irritates the oyster and it responds by coating the grain with layers of saliva and calcium. The oyster and its pearl provide a beautiful picture of a positive response to life's irritants.

Going through trying times is not pleasant. Many Christians naively think that if they obey the Lord, they will be spared from any trials. When trials hit them, they are confused and often angry at God. Yet the Bible says:

...do not be surprised at the fiery ordeal among you which comes upon you for your testing, as though some strange thing were happening to you.

1 Peter 4:12 (NASB)

In today's verse, James does not say "*if* you encounter various trials" but "*whenever*". The Bible gives abundant testimony that all of God's saints encounter trials. The purpose of the trial is so that we may be "mature and complete, not lacking anything". J.B. Phillips understood this as he paraphrased the passage:

When all kinds of trials crowd into your lives, my brothers, don't resent them as intruders, but welcome them as friends! Realise that they have come to test your endurance. But let the

*process go on until that endurance is fully developed, and you
will find you have become men (and women) of mature
character.*

James 1:2-4 (JPB)

God gives us a promise that we can "rejoice in our sufferings, because
we know that suffering produces perseverance; perseverance, character;
and character, hope"[29]. It is through the hurt, pain and ugliness that,
often, God creates beauty in each of us. Let us remember the pearl and
see our irritations and trials in a new light. Let us allow God to develop
something of beauty in us and become mature and complete, not lacking
in anything.

---

[29] Romans 5:3b-4 (NIV)

16

Dress in Humility

And all of you, dress yourselves in humility as you relate to one another, for "God opposes the proud but gives grace to the humble." So humble yourselves under the mighty power of God, and at the right time he will lift you up in honour.

1 Peter 5:5-7 (NLT)

*M*any animals are known for the stereotypes such as the hardworking beaver, the aggressive bull, the stubborn donkey, the elephant who never forgets, the wily fox, the laughing hyena, the quiet mouse, the greedy pig, the cowardly chicken and the proud peacock, distinguished by the long, green iridescent tail that it spreads out like a fan. We have even coined the idiom, "as proud as a peacock".

The world tells us to assert ourselves and put ourselves first. The enemy of our souls wants nothing more than for us to be mired in pride and arrogance. However, the Bible encourages humility. "...dress yourselves in humility as you relate to one another." When Peter tells us to "dress" ourselves in humility, he's using a very interesting word. That word, which he chose for a reason, is tied to the Greek word for a slave's apron. He may have been thinking of that dramatic moment in the upper room just before Jesus was crucified. Jesus laid aside his outer garments, put on a servant's towel and washed their feet concluding with the words:

If I then, your Lord and Master, have washed your feet; ye also ought to wash one another's feet.

John 13:14 (KJV)

Paul used similar terminology in Colossians 3:12:

...you must clothe yourselves with ... humility.

Colossians 3:12 (GNB)

The word "humility" means to walk in a spirit of lowliness. It is the opposite of thinking you are better than others, prideful and arrogant.

Do nothing from selfishness or empty conceit, but with humility of mind regard one another as more important than yourselves.

Philippians 2:3 (NASB)

Genuine humility involves us not thinking too highly of ourselves and requires that we regard one another as more important than ourselves.

It is therefore seen in how we *regard* one another[30] and in how we *relate* to one another.[31]

Have you applied your 'apron' today?

---

[30] See Philippians 2:3
[31] See 1 Peter 5:5

17

Don't Whittle While It's White

"You know the saying, 'Four months between planting and harvest.' But I say, wake up and look around. The fields are already ripe for harvest."

John 4:35 (NLT)

*R*ecently I stumbled across a list of composers who have created some of the most beautiful and complex music the world has ever known. But they also had extreme eccentricities which led to some decidedly odd behaviour. One such was Erik Satie. The nineteenth-century French composer Erik Satie is best known for his piano suite *Trois Gymnopedies*. But did you know that Satie owned twelve identical grey, velvet suits, wearing just one repeatedly until it wore out, at which time he would begin wearing another? More remarkable than this was his diet, which consisted of nothing but foods which were white: eggs, sugar, shredded bones, animal fat, veal, salt, coconuts, rice, pasta, turnips, chicken cooked in white water, white cheese, cotton salad and certain kinds of fish.

In John 4 we find Jesus spending a significant amount of time talking to a Samaritan woman about her personal life, answering her spiritual questions, and treating her with dignity and respect. The words of our verse today come on the heels of her witness to her community. When she returned to her village, she told the people:

Come, see a man, which told me all things that ever I did: is not this the Christ?

John 4:29 (KJV)

This woman so enthusiastically shared her testimony of Jesus that the entire village of Sychar went out of the city to find Him.[32] Jesus then tells the disciples:

---

[32] See John 4:30

Do you not say, It is still four months until harvest time comes? Look! I tell you, raise your eyes and observe the fields and see how they are already white for harvesting.

John 4:35 (AMPC)

White for harvesting? What does that mean? When the corn fields were ripe for harvesting, they looked white, but Jesus was speaking spiritually of a harvest of souls. As He spoke, He was approached by a whole group of people including the Samaritan woman and the men she met in town. One scholar has noted that workers in these small villages were known to wear white workers' garments. This village of workers was so affected by the Samaritan woman's testimony that they dropped what they were doing and immediately went to see Jesus, still dressed in their white workers' garments. When the Lord saw a crowd of people coming toward Him dressed in white, He didn't just see white garments; He saw a harvest that was white and ready to be reaped among the Samaritans.

Many Samaritans from that town believed in Him because of the woman's testimony.

John 4:39 (ESV)

Raise your eyes and observe; see how the fields are already white for harvesting. Look around you and see your community, your neighbourhood and your workmates. See the urgency of the hour. Don't whittle your time while the fields are white. What are you going to do about the whitened fields all around you?

18

Tracking Our Tears

You keep track of all my sorrows. You have collected all my tears in your bottle. You have recorded each one in your book.

Psalm 56:8 (NLT)

Over the years I have collected autographs, stamps, coins, postcards and teddy bears. But let's look at a selection of people who possess some of the world's largest collections of the most bizarre things.

- Jean-François Vernetti from Switzerland has collected 11,111 different 'Do Not Disturb' signs from hotels in 189 countries across the world.
- Lorenzo Pescini of Italy has a collection of 8,650 different bottled water labels from 185 different countries and 1,683 different springs.
- Becky Martz has amassed banana stickers consisting of over 7,000 unique labels.
- Dutch collector Niek Vermeulen has 6,290 airsick bags from 1,191 different airlines and almost 200 countries.

God Himself collects something very unusual. Psalm 56:8 tells us what it is.

You keep track of all my sorrows. You have collected all my tears in your bottle. You have recorded each one in your book.

Psalm 56:8 (NLT)

God knows the tears you have shed. He documents every tear and lament. He notices and He records each single tear. Maybe no-one else has noticed; maybe you are in your room alone and you shed a tear in private – God still knows. Often in the Psalms David pours out his heart to God. Sometimes he cries because of his own circumstances; for example:

I'm on a diet of tears – tears for breakfast, tears for supper.

Psalm 42:3 (MSG)

Sometimes he cries because of others:

Streams of tears flow from my eyes, for your law is not obeyed.

Psalm 119:136 (NIV)

Whatever the reason, God keeps track of your tears. He bottles them.

Some people talk about bottling up their tears because they are afraid to let go, to grieve or show emotion; that's not healthy and only leads to an inner pressure cooker of pain. When we are honest with God and express our tears, He can help us. He tells us, "Cast your burden on the Lord." We have a Father who keeps track of all our sorrows and catches every single tear we cry. When we begin to grasp the depth of that truth, we can say with confidence just as David did:

This I know: God is on my side!

Psalm 56:9 (NLT)

19

The 40 Shades of Green

The righteous man will flourish like the palm tree,
He will grow like a cedar in Lebanon.
Planted in the house of the LORD,
They will flourish in the courts of our God.
They will still yield fruit in old age;
They shall be full of sap and very green.

Psalm 92:12-14 (NASB)

*T*he Forty Shades of Green' is a term associated with the beautiful island where I live. It originated in 1959 when Johnny Cash wrote a song of that name while on a trip to Ireland. This land is also known as the Emerald Isle, and renowned for the 'Wearing of the Green'. I'm not sure if there are *forty* shades of green here. I remember from art at school that there are different shades of green such as viridian, olive, mint, jade, lime, apple, avocado, bottle green, emerald, Cadmium Green and Prussian Green. But *forty?*

The colour green represents freshness, life, flourishing, fruitfulness, vibrancy and being full of sap. It reminds me of Psalm 92 where the righteous are described in verse 14 as being "full of sap and very green". How does this happen? It tells us in the previous verse, "…they will flourish in the courts of our God." It is in His courts, in His presence, that we flourish! It is in close relationship to Him. No wonder the Psalmist said in Psalm 84:

How lovely is your dwelling place,
O LORD Almighty!
My soul yearns, even faints,
  for the courts of the LORD;
  my heart and my flesh cry out for the living God …
Better is one day in your courts than a thousand elsewhere.

Psalm 84:10 (NIV)

We flourish and stay fresh and green when we are vitally connected with our Lord, abiding in His Word and walking in His ways. Without Him, we can neither live, nor grow, much less will we flourish and bear fruit! But notice in our psalm today the lovely words "flourish", "fruit" and "full of sap".

Stay fresh and green. Stay connected.

20

God's Will

Because he holds fast to me in love, I will deliver him; I will protect him, because he knows my name. When he calls to me, I will answer him; I will be with him in trouble; I will rescue him and honour him. With long life I will satisfy him and show him my salvation.

Psalm 91:14-16 (ESV)

I recall in my early formative years dragging around my childhood "blankie". It was bubblegum pink, edged with soft shimmering satin, and I experienced severe withdrawal symptoms when it had to undergo the wash cycle. That tattered old blanket was a source of security and comfort, especially when visiting new places and people.

Psalm 91 offers security to all of us. It is spoken to those who live "in the shelter of the Most High"[33]. The specific words in verses 14-16 are addressed to anyone who sets their love on the Lord and knows His Name. None of us are immune to difficulty, but in the midst of our troubled waters, God says something remarkable and well worth memorising:

- "I will deliver him..." (cause to escape);
- "I will protect him..." (set on high);
- "I will answer him..." (respond to prayer, speak);
- "I will be with him in trouble..." (in afflictions, in distress);
- "I will rescue him..." (bring into safety, set free);
- "...and honour him..." (make rich, strong, heavy with honour);
- "With long life I will satisfy him..." (have abundance in the journey);
- "and show him my salvation" (victory, welfare, eternal life).

---

[33] Psalm 91:1 (AMP)

Enjoy the "secret place"[34]. Allow God to be your source of strength, hope and encouragement today. Take comfort and draw your security from your covenant relationship with Him.

---

[34] Psalm 91:1 (NKJV)

21

Here Am I

Then I heard the voice of the Lord, saying, "Whom shall I send, and who will go for Us?" Then I said, "Here am I. Send me!"

Isaiah 6:8 (AMP)

What led to the declaration of these words? It all started with Isaiah's *primary* vision. Isaiah saw God. This was no shallow or superficial view of God. He had a spectacular revelation or disclosure of God being the absolute and supreme ruler and king. This vision of God's sovereignty was strongly accompanied by seeing God as both being holy and glorious!

I saw the Lord sitting on a throne, lofty and exalted, with the train of His robe filling the temple ... Holy, Holy, Holy, is the LORD of hosts...The whole earth is full of His glory.

Isaiah 6:1-3 (NASB)

Greg Haslam, in his book *A Radical Encounter With God*, says this:

We must rid ourselves of all degraded and diminished concepts of God. If we, as a Church, are to become a force to be reckoned with in the earth then we must see afresh what God is really like.

Following on from his primary vision of God, Isaiah experienced a *personal* vision. That was where he saw himself warts and all. When Isaiah saw the Lord, he instantly realised that there were problems within his own heart. In verse 5, Isaiah succinctly related his own response to seeing God in his glory.

"Woe is me, for I am ruined! Because I am a man of unclean lips, and I live among a people of unclean lips; for my eyes have seen the King, the LORD of hosts."

Isaiah 6:5 (NASB)

Isaiah didn't go, "*Wow* is me!" He said, "*Woe* is me." "Woe" is not really a word you would hear often today as it has almost vanished from our language. But for the Old Testament prophets it was a potent weapon in their arsenal of words and preceded the most serious of announcements. Even Jesus used it of the teachers of the law and the Pharisees. Isaiah's outward respectability crumbled as he saw his inner decadence. But God forgave him and made him totally clean.

It was then that he perceived the *people* vision and uttered the following words:

> *And then I heard the voice of the Master:*
>   *"Whom shall I send?*
>   *Who will go for us?"*
> *I spoke up,*
>   *"I'll go.*
>   *Send me!"*
> *He said, "Go and tell this people..."*

Isaiah 6:8-9 (MSG)

Isaiah wanted to be the answer to God's question. How about us? God is still looking for people who have been so moved by His majesty, and have experienced His mercy on a personal basis, that they will be eager to join in His mission.

22

Talking Nonsense

Set a guard, O LORD, over my mouth; keep watch over the door of my lips!

Psalm 141:3 (ESV)

Apparently, the English language has ninety-eight words for talking nonsense. What does that say about us? Having filtered the lengthy list, here are a few samples: babble, balderdash, baloney, blarney, blather, claptrap, codswallop, gibberish, hogwash, palaver, prattle, twaddle and waffle.

Interestingly the Bible lays great emphasis on our words and our use of the tongue. I remember my childhood visits to the doctor. I could never understand why he always wanted to see my tongue when the reason I was there was a stomach ache. Later in life I learned there was wisdom behind his words, "Let me see your tongue." It can reveal telltale signs of anaemia, dehydration, kidney problems and infections. The colour and coating on a tongue can also be an effective way of spotting symptoms too.

"Let me see your tongue" is even more true as a test of spiritual health and wellbeing. Our words are symptomatic of the state of our hearts. The tongue is the courier of the thoughts of the heart. Jesus made that clear in Matthew 12:

> *"A good man out of the good treasure of his heart brings forth good things, and an evil man out of the evil treasure brings forth evil things. But I say to you that for every idle word men may speak, they will give account of it in the day of judgment."*

> *Matthew 12:35-36 (NKJV)*

The tongue is the infallible index of the heart, the gauge that accurately reads our spiritual temperature. The word Jesus used for "idle" is *argos,* meaning 'useless, purposeless, profitless'.

By contrast, our words should be edifying, as Paul told us:

Let no foul or polluting language, nor evil word nor unwholesome or worthless talk [ever] come out of your mouth, but only such [speech] as is good and beneficial to the spiritual progress of others, as is fitting to the need and the occasion, that it may be a blessing and give grace (God's favour) to those who hear it.

Ephesians 4:29 (AMPC)

May our words edify others and impact grace. May today's scripture from the Psalms be our daily prayer.

23

Whoever – Whatever – Whenever

So Jesus answered and said to them, "Have faith in God. For assuredly, I say to you, whoever says to this mountain, 'Be removed and be cast into the sea,' and does not doubt in his heart, but believes that those things he says will be done, he will have whatever he says. Therefore I say to you, whatever things you ask when you pray, believe that you receive them, and you will have them. And whenever you stand praying, if you have anything against anyone, forgive him, that your Father in heaven may also forgive you your trespasses."

Mark 11:22-25 (NKJV)

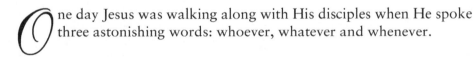ne day Jesus was walking along with His disciples when He spoke three astonishing words: whoever, whatever and whenever.

WHOEVER

"Truly I tell you, whoever says to this mountain..." I love the 'whoever' references in the Bible. God could easily have limited the scope but He used the all-inclusive word "whoever" in several passages. None is blocked or barred. For example:

For God so loved the world that He gave His only begotten Son, that whoever believes in Him should not perish but have everlasting life.

John 3:16 (NKJV)

Whoever drinks of the water that I shall give him will never thirst.

John 4:14 (NKJV)

Whoever hears these sayings of Mine, and does them, I will liken him to a wise man who built his house on the rock.

Matthew 7:24 (NKJV)

WHATEVER

"Whatever things you ask when you pray, believe that you receive them, and you will have them."

Now this is the confidence that we have in Him, that if we ask anything according to His will, He hears us. And if we know that He hears us, whatever we ask, we know that we have the petitions that we have asked of Him.

1 John 5:14-15 (NKJV)

God's Word reveals His will. Jesus made it clear:

"If you live in Me [abide vitally united to Me] and My words remain in you and continue to live in your hearts, ask whatever you will, and it shall be done for you."

John 15:7 (AMPC)

WHENEVER

"Whenever you stand praying, if you have anything against anyone, forgive him, that your Father in heaven may also forgive you your trespasses." Jesus is not changing the subject here. He is still talking about prayer. He now links it with forgiveness. Many people ruin their health and their lives by taking the poison of bitterness, resentment and unforgiveness. Wounds can fester into infections if left untreated. That's exactly how unforgiveness works. Whatever was done to us pierced our skin, but if we keep prying it open and looking at the wound, it won't be able to heal. Don't sabotage your prayers by harbouring unforgiveness in your heart.

24

Walk of Faith

For we live by faith, not by sight.

2 Corinthians 5:7 (NIV)

*H*ave you heard of the Hollywood walk of fame? It is the world's most famous sidewalk containing over 2,500 terrazzo and brass stars embedded in the pavement bearing the names of Hollywood's biggest celebrities past and present. It has appeared in iconic movies such as *Pretty Woman* and is visited by over ten million tourists each year.

Hebrews 11 could be called the "walk of faith" because it showcases dozens of great men and women and relates their exploits, giving snippets of their lives. We encounter names such as Abel, Enoch, Noah, Abraham, Isaac, Jacob, Sara, Joseph, Moses, Rahab, Gideon, Barak, Samson, Jephthah, David, Samuel and the prophets. Verses 32-34 elaborate by saying:

> *And what more shall I say? For time will fail me if I tell of Gideon, Barak, Samson, Jephthah, of David and Samuel and the prophets, who by faith conquered kingdoms, performed acts of righteousness, obtained promises, shut the mouths of lions, quenched the power of fire, escaped the edge of the sword, from weakness were made strong, became mighty in war, put foreign armies to flight.*

Hebrews 11:32-34 (AMP)

All of the examples walked by faith. In Verse 2 we are told:

> *The act of faith is what distinguished our ancestors, set them above the crowd.*

Hebrews 11:2 (MSG)

They are not defined by their flaws; they are defined by their faith. They are simply 'whoevers' who chose to operate on whatever God said.

This wonderful chapter is an example to us on how we can, and should, have faith in God as well.

God's will is that we live by faith. Walking by faith requires a strong determination to follow God's plan regardless of what life throws your way. He has promised that He will be with you every single step, walking with you, carrying you, supporting you. It is a journey of tremendous blessing and reward.

25

Nobodies in God's Nobility

If the foot says, "Because I am not a hand, I am not a part of the body," it is not for this reason any the less a part of the body. And if the ear says, "Because I am not an eye, I am not a part of the body," it is not for this reason any the less a part of the body.

1 Corinthians 12:15-16 (NASB)

I wonder if you know the answers to the following questions. Who visited D.L. Moody at the shoe store where he worked and shared the gospel with him? Who was the little elderly woman who prayed faithfully for Billy Graham for many years? Who financed William Carey's ministry to India? Which great theological mind influenced Martin Luther and became his confidant and friend? Which substitute lay preacher stepped into the pulpit and read Isaiah 45:22 influencing the future of Charles Haddon Spurgeon? Which author wrote a book which impacted the life of John Newton? Who looked after Paul in the dungeon as he penned his last letter to Timothy? Who were the four faithful friends who brought the paralytic man to Jesus on a stretcher?

How did you do? Most people don't know the answers. However, without these unknown people, a lot of what we call church history would be missing. A lot of lives would have been untouched. These anonymous people were a very necessary part of the Body of Christ. It doesn't matter if we do not remember their names – we know their impact even today. People like Kimball, Pearle Goode, Melanchthon, Onesiphorus and the anonymous heroes of faith remind us that we all have purpose in the great plan of God.

Paul said:

And some of the parts that seem weakest and least important are really the most necessary.

1 Corinthians 12:22 (TLB)

Be encouraged.

26

The Golden Rule

Treat men exactly as you would like them to treat you.

Luke 6:31 (JBP)

*I*n the verse above, Jesus gives us a general rule on how to treat people. Perhaps you have heard of 'The Law of Echoes'. It is the story of a boy who called out to the surrounding mountains, "I love you," and was comforted to hear the words echo around the mountains and come back to him again and again. One day when he was angry, he yelled, "I hate you," and found that those words also came back to him again and again.

And so it is in life. Jesus told us:

> *Treat men exactly as you would like them to treat you ... Don't judge other people and you will not be judged yourselves. Don't condemn and you will not be condemned. Make allowances for others and people will make allowances for you. Give and men will give to you – yes, good measure, pressed down, shaken together and running over will they pour into your lap. For whatever measure you use with other people, they will use in their dealings with you.*

Luke 6:31,37-38 (JBP)

This is known as the 'Golden Rule'. How do you like to be treated? Most people reply to this question by saying that they want to be treated justly and with fairness; to be treated kindly and graciously; to be given respect, dignity and shown consideration; to be appreciated and valued. But how do we treat others? Do we show them the same respect, kindness, grace, justice and dignity?

We as Christians should echo the same love and respect God has shown us. The Bible says:

> *As I have loved you, so you must love one another.*

John 13:34 (JBP)

Accept one another, then, just as Christ accepted you.

Romans 15:7 (NIV)

Be kind and compassionate to one another, forgiving each other, just as in Christ God forgave you.

Ephesians 4:32 (NIV)

In light of that, let's apply the Golden Rule as we step out today. As Peter tells us:

Treat everyone you meet with dignity.

1 Peter 2:17 (MSG)

27

Roll and Repose

Commit your way to the Lord (roll and repose each care of your load on Him) trust (lean on, rely on, and be confident) also in Him and He will bring it to pass.

Psalm 37:5 (AMPC)

*T*he word used for "commit" in Hebrew is *galal*. It is an interesting word found also in Proverbs 16:3:

Roll your works upon the Lord (commit and trust them wholly to Him; He will cause your thoughts to become agreeable to His will, and) so shall your plans be established and succeed.

Proverbs 16:3 (AMPC)

The word "commit" is a picture of a camel with a load. Camels were an important source of transportation in the Middle East. The camel drivers had a command: *"Galal!"* At this loud command the camels would kneel down and roll over on their sides so their master could unload or free the load. What a picture for us. We can kneel down in prayer and roll our cares at His feet. Roll and repose.

The theme of Psalm 37 is, "Do not fret." God does not want us carrying anxiety and burdens in our hearts. His desire is that we offload each and every one of them to Him. As Peter said:

Casting the whole of your care [all your anxieties, all your worries, all your concerns, once and for all] on Him, for He cares for you affectionately and cares about you watchfully.

1 Peter 5:7 (AMPC)

C.H. Spurgeon's exposition of verse 5 is instructive:

Commit thy way unto the Lord. Roll the whole burden of life upon the Lord. Leave with Jehovah not thy present fretfulness merely, but all thy cares; in fact, submit the whole tenor of thy way to him. Cast away anxiety, resign thy will, submit thy judgment, leave all with the God of all.

How many of us are carrying loads we need to give to God?

28

The Unfolding of Your Words

The unfolding of Your words gives light; It gives understanding to the simple.

Psalm 119:130 (NASB)

*P*salm 119 is the longest chapter in the Bible. It has 176 verses. It is full of praise and adoration for Scripture. There is so much here that Charles Spurgeon spent about 350 pages discussing this one psalm in his classic, *The Treasury of David.*

A story is told of a man who loved old books. He met an acquaintance who had just thrown away a Bible that had been stored in the attic of his ancestral home for generations.

"I couldn't read it," the friend explained. "Somebody named Guten-something had printed it."

"Not Gutenberg!" the book lover exclaimed in horror. "That Bible was one of the first books ever printed. Why, a copy just sold for over two million dollars!"

His friend was unimpressed. "Mine wouldn't have brought a dollar. Some fellow named Martin Luther had scribbled all over it in German."

Do we realise the worth of the Word of God? I have several different copies at home, plus one in the glove compartment of my car. Interlinears, paraphrases, annotated, amplified and study Bibles, leather-bound, hard-bound, paperback, large print, red letter, wide margin, and many other renderings of the Bible abound. We have a treasure trove within easy reach, but do we mine for its nuggets of gold?

The entrance and unfolding of Your words give light; their unfolding gives understanding (discernment and comprehension) to the simple.

Psalm 119:130 (AMPC)

In the complex world in which we live, we desperately need God's wisdom for making sound decisions. We need insight for living. In Luke

24 the two men on the Emmaus road were reminiscing about how they had met the Saviour and how He had walked and talked with them. They said to each other:

> *"Were not our hearts burning within us while He talked with us on the road and opened the Scriptures to us?"*
>
> *Luke 24:32 (NIV)*

May our hearts burn within us today as we allow His Word entrance into our hearts. May we receive its light and gain understanding for our lives.

29

Firsts

But I have this against you, that you have left your first love.

Revelation 2:4 (NASB)

- The first song to be sung in outer space was *Happy Birthday* on 8 March 1969.
- The first toothbrush was invented in China in 1498.
- Britain's very first mobile phone call was made on 1 January 1985 by Ernie Wise.
- Lego was first invented in Denmark in 1949. The pieces were originally called Automatic Binding Bricks.
- Laika was the name of the first dog in space.

There are many firsts in life. The Bible speaks specifically of our "first love" (*protos agape*). It is mentioned in the book of Revelation when Jesus was addressing the Ephesian believers. When Paul wrote to the Ephesian believers (probably around AD 54), he mentioned their love for one another[35] and encouraged loving unity in the body of Christ. [36] But later, God warned the Ephesians that they had left their "first love"[37]. Jesus praised the church in Ephesus for their works, labour, patience and perseverance[38]. But He warned:

...I have this [charge] against you, that you have left your first love [you have lost the depth of love that you first had for Me].

Revelation 2:4 (AMP)

In other words, "You have left the love that should be the most important and number one priority in your life." Or, as He taught in Mark 12:

---

[35] See Ephesians 1:15-16
[36] See Ephesians 4:15-16
[37] See Revelation 2:1-7
[38] See Revelation 2:1-3

"Love the Lord your God with all your heart, with all your soul, with all your mind and with all your strength."

Mark 12:30

I would imagine that many of the Ephesian believers were in a state of shock when they first read this letter. "What does He mean – we have left our first love? Doesn't He see all we're doing?" But motion is no substitute for emotion and devotion to Him.

John, author of Revelation, is one who really understood God's love. At one time he and his brother James had been known as the "Sons of Thunder"[39]. Apparently, they were very quick-tempered and were quick to judge others. Yet Christ had dramatically changed John's heart and as you read through the New Testament you discover that one out of every three verses on the subject of love was penned by John. He changed from a Son of Thunder into an apostle of love.

Have you lost the depth of love that you first had for Jesus?

---

[39] Mark 3:17 (AMPC)

30

Surely the Lord is in This Place

Then Jacob awoke from his sleep and said, "Surely the Lord
is in this place, and I did not know it."

Genesis 28:16 (NKJV)

*P*earl Bailey said, "People see God every day, they just don't recognise Him." We sleep through much of our life, simply ignorant of all that the Lord is doing for us, unaware of His presence and leading. The above verse tells us of when Jacob awoke to reality and discovered the Lord's presence with him.

There is a difference between saying "God is everywhere" and saying "God is here". The Psalmist stated:

> *...Where can I flee from your presence?*
> *If I go up to the heavens, you are there;*
> *if I make my bed in the depths, you are there.*

Psalm 139:7-8 (NIV)

God is everywhere present. But He is also here with us, "in this place". God wants to relate to each one of us – even Jacob.

Jacob was living his life as if God were not there. He had deceived his father and stolen the birthright and the blessing from his brother. He was running from his brother Esau and was caught between a rock and a hard place. His past was a mess and his future uncertain. In that unexpected, lonely, hard place Jacob realised God was there. He declared, "How awesome is this place!"

In a testing time the Psalmist also said:

> *God is our refuge and strength,*
> *A very present help in trouble.*

Psalm 46:1 (NKJV)

To be aware of the presence of God is the most beautiful, adventurous experience in a person's life. He is closer than our very breath. In fact:

...in Him we live and move and have our being...

Acts 17:28 (NKJV)

May we 'awake' to a full awareness of God's promise, provision and presence in our lives!

April

May

May

1

The Wind and the Winnow

And suddenly there came from heaven a sound like a mighty rushing wind, and it filled the entire house where they were sitting.

Acts 2:2 (ESV)

Wind is invisible, ethereal, mysterious and powerful. The Beaufort scale, which is used in the Met Office forecasts, is an empirical measure for describing wind intensity. It was originally invented by Admiral Beaufort in the 1700s. Many marine forecasts still give the wind's strength using the Beaufort scale. There are a variety of tools to determine the direction of the wind such as a simple weathervane or an anemometer.

Acts 2:2 records that when the Holy Spirit was given, the display of ability and power astounded everyone present. The intensity was documented: "a mighty rushing wind". The direction was also chronicled: "there came from heaven". While wind is invisible, we can see its effects as it rustles a tree full of foliage and so it is with the Holy Spirit. Just as we know that the wind is present when the boat's sail is full, when the kite soars upward, and when the windmill is turning, we know that the Holy Spirit is active when we see the typical effects of His works and the fruit produced.

The word "Spirit" is translated from the Greek term *pneuma* which literally means 'breath, a current of air or breeze'. The Hebrew word for 'Spirit' (*ruach*) also means 'breath'. The English word 'Spirit' comes from the Latin verb *spirare* which means 'to breathe'. This is a theme that runs throughout the entire Bible. In the book of Genesis, we see God breathing life into Adam and Eve.[40] In the book of Ezekiel we see God breathing life into the field of dry bones.[41] In the book of John we see Jesus

---

[40] See Genesis 2:6-7
[41] See Ezekiel 37:9-14

breathing the Holy Spirit upon the disciples.[42] He is the Wind of Heaven, the Breath of God. A well-loved hymn states:

> *Breathe on me, Breath of God,*
> *Fill me with life anew,*
> *That I may love the way you love,*
> *And do what you would do.*

In Acts 1:4 Jesus calls the Holy Spirit the gift of the Father. Let us be thankful for the gift of the Holy Spirit. Let us give thanks for the quickening work of the Holy Spirit in our lives.[43] As regenerated, indwelt and sanctified by the Holy Spirit, may we continually yield to the Holy Spirit and be changed from glory into glory. As the wind blows away the chaff in the natural discarding refuse of winnowed corn, so may the Holy Spirit blow away the chaff, ungodly refuse and carnality, of our lives this Pentecost.

---

[42] See John 20:19-22
[43] See John 6:63

2

Brand Name

So for a whole year Barnabas and Saul met with the church and taught great numbers of people. The disciples were called Christians first at Antioch.

Acts 11:26 (NIV)

ave you ever looked at a brand name and wondered about its origin? Here are a few interesting ones:

- *Harpic:* from the first three letters of the first name and surname of the man who developed it – Harry Pickup.
- *Ryvita:* from the word 'rye' and the Latin for life, *vita.*
- *7-Up:* named by the inventor who had already rejected six names for his product.
- *Amazon.com:* Jeff Bezos wanted a name for his company that began with 'A' so that it would appear early in alphabetical order. He began looking through the dictionary and settled on 'amazon' because it was a river he considered the biggest in the world, as he hoped his company would be.
- *Starbucks:* named after Starbuck, a character in Herman Melville's novel *Moby Dick.*
- *Hovis:* derives from the Latin words, *hominis vis* meaning 'man's strength'.
- *Lego:* from the Danish words *leg godt* meaning 'play well'.

Our verse today uses the term "Christian" and shows its origin. The word is only used three times in the New Testament. The other references are in Acts 26:28 and 1 Peter 4:16.

Then Agrippa said to Paul, 'Do you think that in such a short time you can persuade me to be a Christian?'

Acts 26:28 (NIVUK)

> *However, if you suffer as a Christian, do not be ashamed, but praise God that you bear that name.*
>
> *1 Peter 4:16 (NIVUK)*

In each instance the Greek word *christianos* is used, derived from the word *christos* which means 'Christ, the anointed one'. A Christian, then, is someone who is a follower of Christ. In our day there is a certain casualness about 'following' someone. It's what you do on Twitter. But in the Bible, to follow Christ was to believe in Christ, side with His party and follow His example. The word was initially used by their detractors in a derogatory sense, but believers embraced the term as a badge of honour. As Peter phrased it, "...praise God that you bear that name."

Today as we go about our business, let's remember that we bear the name of Christ and people form their opinions about Him from what they see and hear from us. Let's represent Him worthily and well.

3

Don't Overlook the Little Things

And a poor widow came and put in two small copper coins, which make a penny.

Mark 12:42 (ESV)

While browsing online recently I stumbled upon a list of things which I didn't know had names. Here are a few examples for you to try out.

- *Aglet* – the metal or plastic coating on the end of a shoelace.
- *Buccula* – a person's double chin.
- *Glabella* – the space between your eyebrows.
- *Nurdle* – the term for the small dab of toothpaste you put on your toothbrush.
- *Drupelets* – the bumps on raspberries.
- *Vibrissae* – a cat's whiskers.
- *Ferrule* – the metal band on top of a pencil which holds the rubber in place.
- *Tines* – the prongs on a fork.

Jesus noticed the little things. One day, He was sitting with His disciples near the temple treasury watching people depositing money into the offering receptacles. He watched as the rich were contributing large sums of money, but then along came a widow with two small coins in her hand. The ESV calls them "two small copper coins, which make a penny"[44]. The KJV calls the coins "mites". These were the smallest denomination of coins. The widow put her coins into the box, and Jesus called His disciples to Himself and pointed out her action:

"Truly I say to you, this poor widow put in more than all the contributors to the treasury; for they all put in out of their

---

[44] Mark 12:42

surplus, but she, out of her poverty, put in all she owned, all she had to live on."

Mark 12:43-44 (NASB)

Jesus saw what no one else did: He saw the humble gift of a poor widow. He saw not just the portion but the proportion of her giving.

He also observed the cup of cold water.

"And if you give even a cup of cold water to one of the least of my followers, you will surely be rewarded."

Matthew 10:42 (NLT)

A cup of cold water is no big deal to us – it is simple and inexpensive – but Jesus sees it and remembers it. He told us:

"I was thirsty and you gave Me something to drink."

Matthew 25:35 (AMPC)

He explained this by saying:

"Whatever you did for one of the least of these brothers of mine, you did for me."

Matthew 25:40 (HCSB)

Don't overlook or dismiss the little things. God sees them all. The everyday kingdom of God is built on small moments of servanthood, thoughtfulness and kindness.

4

Without Complaining

Do everything without complaining and arguing.

The following is an astonishing yet genuine list of complaints made by holidaymakers to their travel agent:

- "I think it should be explained in the brochure that the local store does not sell proper biscuits like custard creams or ginger nuts."
- "The beach was too sandy."
- "We booked an excursion to a water park but no-one told us we had to bring our swimming costumes and towels."
- "No-one told us there would be fish in the sea. The children were startled."
- "Although the brochure said that there was a fully equipped kitchen, there was no egg-slicer in the drawers."
- "We had to queue outside with no air conditioning."
- "The street signs weren't in English. I don't understand how anyone can get around."

Do we ridiculously give verbal expression to our daily frustrations and vent our exasperations? Or perhaps air our grievances on social media? While complaining seems to be the norm for our society, it should never be part of our lives. Paul wrote:

In everything you do, stay away from complaining and arguing so that no one can speak a word of blame against you. You are to live clean, innocent lives as children of God in a dark world full of people who are crooked and stubborn.

Shine out among them like beacon lights, holding out to them the Word of Life.

Philippians 2:14-16 (TLB)

The Greek word for "complaining" is *goggusmos* which means 'expressing one's discontent'. Spurgeon offers an antidote for a complaining, murmuring spirit, writing:

If we complained less, and praised more, we should be happier, and God would be more glorified. Let us daily praise God for common mercies – common as we frequently call them, and yet so priceless, that when deprived of them we are ready to perish. Let us bless God for the eyes with which we behold the sun, for the health and strength to walk abroad, for the bread we eat, for the raiment we wear. Let us praise him that we are not cast out among the hopeless, or confined amongst the guilty; let us thank him for liberty, for friends, for family associations and comforts; let us praise him, in fact, for everything which we receive from his bounteous hand, for we deserve little, and yet are most plenteously endowed.

Complaining is draining and never changes our situations. Stay positive and prioritise praise.

5

A Packed Lunch

"There's a young boy here with five barley loaves and two fish. But what good is that with this huge crowd?"

John 6:9 (NLT)

*M*y school mates were reminiscing recently over a cup of coffee on their memories of unpalatable school dinners. What was your school dinner experience? Did anyone have a good one? Those of a certain age will remember spam fritters. Even to this day, when I think about them I cringe. The salty spam slab of processed meat was covered in a thick layer of truly awful batter and deep-fried – maybe just soaked? – in oil until the grease level went off the charts. Then there was the stewed sausage drowned in gelatinous onion gravy accompanied by the chemistry set taste of instant mash. I dreaded the weekly appearance of the watery, overcooked, rank-smelling grey cauliflower they served up in the lumpy wallpaper paste which masqueraded as cheese sauce. However, while my friends thought otherwise, I still have fond memories of the puddings. The lovely creamy custard could make even the prospect of double afternoon physics bearable. Blancmange with prunes; pink custard; semolina and rosehip syrup... delectable! At our table we used to share our lunches. I would readily exchange a spam fritter for four prunes!

In John 6 we read of a young boy who willingly shared his lunch. Five thousand people were waiting to be fed. The loaves given were not big, long loaves of bread. Rather, they were small round pieces of flat bread the size of biscuits today. And the fish were not trophy bass, but rather sardine-like in size. When the young boy's mom packed his lunch bag that day, she had no idea of its significance and the miracle which lay ahead. Jesus took those little biscuits and sardines and they were multiplied in His hands. He just kept on breaking them and giving them to His disciples, and the loaves and fish kept on multiplying. He kept breaking and giving until every person in the crowd had no more desire for food. And when the disciples took of the leftovers, there were twelve baskets full. One for every doubting disciple!

That little boy received back from his generosity more than he could carry home. Let's remember that little is always much in the hands of Christ.

6

A Few Choice Words

A word fitly spoken is like apples of gold in a setting of silver.

Proverbs 25:11 (ESV)

Do more than exist, live.
Do more than touch, feel.
Do more than look, observe.
Do more than read, absorb.
Do more than hear, listen.
Do more than thank, ponder.
Do more than talk, say something.

John H. Rhoads

Do more than talk, say something. Are your words "fitly spoken"? The word "fitly" is an interesting term in the Hebrew. It involves the idea of timing – a word spoken *at the right time*, or a word *well-timed*. It is also related to the idea of a wheel, such as a potter's wheel – a *well-turned* or *well-formed* word. As the NASB puts it:

Like apples of gold in settings of silver
Is a word spoken in right circumstances.

Proverbs 25:11 (NASB)

A word "fitly spoken" can brighten the day for anyone you know. On the other hand, all it takes is the wrong word to inflict pain and anxiety. There is a similar statement in Proverbs 16:24:

Pleasant words are like a honeycomb,
Sweetness to the soul and health to the bones.

Proverbs 16:24 (NKJV)

Today if someone says 'a few choice words', it is usually a euphemistic way to refer to naughty, harsh, denunciatory, brazen or otherwise unsuitable-for-polite-company words. However, the Bible tells us to choose our words wisely and speak 'a few choice words' in season.

> To make an apt answer is a joy to a man, and a word in season, how good it is!
>
> *Proverbs 15:23 (ESV)*

We can purposely order our conversation and speak carefully chosen words of God to produce not only victory in our own lives but in the lives of others as well. Everyone thrives on encouragement and a word spoken in season. Today choose your words wisely and speak life, healing and blessing.

7

Meditate Day and Night

But they delight in doing everything God wants them to, and day and night are always meditating on his laws and thinking about ways to follow him more closely. They are like trees along a riverbank bearing luscious fruit each season without fail. Their leaves shall never wither, and all they do shall prosper.

Psalm 1:2-3 (TLB)

We all want our lives to be like that tree, but did you notice it involves "always meditating"? Meditation is certainly not something new; nor is it New Age. God designed it as a method of pondering on His Word in our hearts and personally applying it to our own lives and circumstances. Instead of emptying our minds, we fill them with the truth of God's Word. It is enlightening our minds with the truth, embracing it and embedding it in our lives. It is intentionally focusing on recalling God's truth that it might resound in our hearts throughout the day and become the grid through which we sift and measure our thoughts and actions.

God promises good success and a prosperous way to a person who meditates on the Word of God. God instructed Joshua that...

This Book of the Law shall not depart from your mouth, but you shall meditate in it day and night, that you may observe to do according to all that is written in it. For then you will make your way prosperous, and then you will have good success.

Joshua 1:8 (NKJV)

David determined:

I will meditate on your precepts and fix my eyes on your ways.

Psalms 119:15 (ESV)

In the Old Testament there are two primary Hebrew words for meditation: *hagah*, which means 'to utter, groan, speak, meditate, or ponder'; and *sihach*, which means 'to muse, rehearse in one's mind, or contemplate'. We literally fill our minds and mouths with God's Word. For example, take a chosen verse and picture it; visualise it in your mind. Then pronounce the verse aloud emphasising different words each time you read it. Next, personalise it by replacing pronouns with your name. It is now time to pray it by turning the verse into a prayer and saying it back to God. Finally, practise it!

Meditating on the Word of God leads to what Paul calls a renewed mind.

> *Do not be conformed to this world, but be transformed by the renewal of your mind, that by testing you may discern what is the will of God, what is good and acceptable and perfect.*
>
> Romans 12:2 (ESV)

No wonder he tells us in Colossians 3:16:

> *Let the Word of Christ dwell in [us] richly…*
>
> Colossians 3:16 (ESV)

8

Responding Rightly When You're Wronged

Live in harmony with one another. Do not be haughty, but associate with the lowly. Never be wise in your own sight. Repay no one evil for evil, but give thought to do what is honourable in the sight of all. If possible, so far as it depends on you, live peaceably with all. Beloved, never avenge yourselves, but leave it to the wrath of God, for it is written, "Vengeance is mine, I will repay," says the Lord.

Romans 12:16-19 (ESV)

*D*on't react; respond. To love others as Christ loved us, we need to respond rather than react to their behaviour. Think about it: reactions are usually self-centred and defensive; they lead to a counter-attack where we unleash how we feel and express what we expect or desire or demand of others. Instead of blindly reacting, we should thoughtfully respond. Saying something out of anger always results in damage.

Refrain from anger and turn from wrath; do not fret – it leads only to evil.

Psalm 37:8 (NIV)

Responses are at the other end of the spectrum: seeing where another person is, and meeting him or her there, with love. Responses involve compassion, insight and a desire for reconciliation that exceeds the desire to win an argument.

Whatever happens, conduct yourselves in a manner worthy of the Gospel of Christ.

Philippians 1:27 (NIV)

In other words, make sure that you respond with a Christ-like attitude. Paul later writes:

You must have the same attitude that Christ Jesus had.

Philippians 2:5 (NLT)

See to it that no one repays evil for evil to anyone, but always pursue what is good for one another and for all.

1 Thessalonians 5:15 (HCSB)

In that little word "see" lies our responsibility. We are to see to it that we do not repay "evil for evil". We are to see to it that we respond in an appropriate manner. We are to see to it that we live in response to God's grace and extend that grace to others. By the grace of God, may we deal with difficult people in love, joy, peace, patience, kindness, goodness, faith, gentleness, and – to top it all off – self-control. May we extend the same love, grace and mercy that God extended to us. And may we be careful not to become the 'difficult people' ourselves!

Are you reacting to your circumstances in the flesh or responding to life's challenges in a Christ-like manner? We are the billboard God wants to use to tell the world about Him. What story are you telling with your reactions or responses?

9

Forgiveness 490

Bear with each other and forgive whatever grievances you may
have against one another. Forgive as the Lord forgave you.

Colossians 3:13 (NIV)

Numbers are one of the significant parts of our lives. I must admit I'm the sort of person who prefers letters to numbers, or English to mathematics. Someone once quipped, "'Mathematics' is an anagram of 'me asthmatic'." That could well describe how I feel when calculating! However, I am interested in mathematical facts. For instance, if you multiply 111,111,111 by 111,111,111, this becomes equal to 12,345,678,987,654,321. You get the pattern 1 to 9 and back to 1 again. Also, the number 2,520 can be divided precisely by 1, 2, 3, 4, 5, 6, 7, 8, 9 and 10.

In Matthew 18 I found the mathematics of forgiveness:

Then Peter came to Him and said, "Lord, how often shall my
brother sin against me, and I forgive him? Up to seven times?"
Jesus said to him, "I do not say to you, up to seven times, but
up to seventy times seven."

Matthew 18:21-22 (NKJV)

Let's do the maths: $7 \times 70 = 490$. The rabbis taught that forgiving up to three times was sufficient, and thus Peter considered he was being more than generous by describing forgiveness as up to seven times. But Jesus insisted that there must be no limits to forgiveness. Jesus was using the numbers to say that you should not put limits on your forgiveness because God has not put limits on forgiveness and mercy toward you.

Jesus' parable of the unforgiving servant follows directly after His "seventy times seven" speech, driving home the point that if we are forgiven the enormous debt of sin against a holy God, how much more should we be eager to forgive those who sin against us, who are just as sinful as we are? The master says in verse 33:

> *"I forgave you that tremendous debt because you pleaded with me. Shouldn't you have mercy on your fellow servant, just as I had mercy on you?"*
>
> *Matthew 18:32-33 (NLT)*

The truth is that we punish ourselves, we cut ourselves off from the free flow of God's grace, when we don't forgive. Nursing even a molehill of a grudge can grow into a smouldering volcano of bitterness. As someone said, "Not forgiving someone is like drinking rat poison and then waiting for the rat to die."

In Colossians 3 Paul has been telling us how to dress for success.

> *So, chosen by God for this new life of love, dress in the wardrobe God picked out for you: compassion, kindness, humility...*
>
> *Colossians 3:12 (MSG)*

Then he mentions the fabric of forgiveness:

> *Forgive as the Lord forgave you.*
>
> *Colossians 3:13 (NIV)*

The verb for "forgive" is *charizomai*, meaning 'to show kindness or favour'. Derived from *charis* (grace), *charizomai* means 'to forgive freely, graciously, not grudgingly, granting to another as a favour'.

May we apply the mathematics of forgiveness to our lives.

10

The Micah Mandate

He has shown you, O man, what is good;
And what does the LORD require of you
But to do justly, to love mercy,
And to walk humbly with your God?

Micah 6:8 (NKJV)

*D*o justly, love mercy and walk humbly. We are saved by grace, through faith and not our works! But God does have an expectation for our lives. It concerns how we treat others.

DO JUSTLY

Live guarding and fighting for a sense of justice on behalf of others. Demonstrate justice in all your dealings with other people. As disciples of Jesus, acting justly means making fair decisions in our business and personal lives. God stamped His image on every human being and we acknowledge that truth when we treat all people with dignity.

His work is perfect,
For all His ways are just;
A God of faithfulness and without injustice,
Righteous and upright is He.

Deuteronomy 32:4 (NKJV)

God is concerned about the protection of foreigners and slaves, of orphans and widows, anyone who is vulnerable and can be easily taken advantage of or wronged. Micah has already attacked injustice in the first three chapters of this book. He has denounced violent acts of physical abuse, confiscation of other people's land and possessions, treating people inhumanely, and cheating other people for financial benefit. The call here is to *do* justice, not just be supportive of justice accomplished by other people. We ourselves are to be people that live out justice. It requires pro-activity on our part.

LOVE MERCY

Reach out to those in need and show God's love for them. Biblical justice is never divorced from acts of love and mercy. Jesus tells us:

> *"Blessed are the merciful, for they shall obtain mercy."*
>
> ???

One day Jesus challenged the Pharisees saying:

> *"Woe to you, teachers of the law and Pharisees, you hypocrites! ... you have neglected the more important matters of the law – justice, mercy and faithfulness. You should have practiced the latter, without neglecting the former."*
>
> *Matthew 23:23 (NIV)*

WALK HUMBLY

The Hebrew root of the word describes a lifestyle that is not proud, not self-willed and not arrogant. We are called to walk in submission to God and to His heart, His will and His ways. A sense of God's presence, an acknowledgement of His love for us, a deep awareness of our need of Him is vital. Walk humbly with your God; not *sometimes* be humble, but *always* walk humbly with your God. D.L. Moody noted this about Moses:

> *...he spent his first forty years being a somebody in Pharaoh's palace; the next forty years being a nobody in the wilderness; the last forty years showing that a nobody can be somebody – with God.*

Let's meditate on the Micah mandate throughout the day, internalise its truth and express it in our lives.

11

What? When? Where?

"No longer will you be called Abram; your name will be Abraham, for I have made you a father of many nations."

Genesis 17:5 (NIV)

*M*y daughter shared with me an interesting fact she noticed on Twitter. If you replace the 'W' in 'What?' 'When?' and 'Where?' with a 'T' you have the answer. What? *That.* When? *Then.* Where? *There.* As I read this, I remembered the slight change in the name Abram to Abraham. In fact, the change is minor, the only difference being one Hebrew letter: ה (pronounced *hey*). The letter *hey* is the fifth letter of the Hebrew alphabet. It represents grace.

Abraham's birth-name 'Abram' means 'exalted father' but God breathes into it – in Hebrew, He adds an aspirate, the single letter *he* – and turns it into a word meaning 'father of a multitude'. Likewise, God also changed the name of Abraham's wife. In order for Abraham to fulfil his mission, he needed his wife by his side in a similarly spiritual level. Therefore, God changed her name from Sarai, which means 'princess', to Sarah meaning the 'mother of nations'. Her name change from Sarai to Sarah was also accomplished by the adding of a *hey* as a suffix. Abraham's new name would forever be a reminder of God's promise to him.

In Genesis 12:2 Abraham was told:

"Then I will make you into a great nation, and I will bless you, and I will make your name great, so that you will exemplify divine blessing."

Genesis 12:2 (NET)

Then a few verses on we read:

"No longer will you be called Abram; your name will be Abraham, for I have made you a father of many nations."

Genesis 17:5 (NIV)

Abraham's new name would forever be a reminder of God's promise to him. Can you imagine the conversation?

"And your name is?"

"Abraham."

"Abraham... um... interesting name. 'Father of a multitude.' Wow! So how many children do you have?"

"Er... well... er... not that many, in a manner of speaking. That is to say, none... at the moment... actually."

What is it that God wants to accomplish in me today that is quite beyond all possibility? Take God at His Word and allow the very infusion of His breath to fill your life and accomplish His plans for you. As the old hymn says, "Breathe on me, Breath of God."

12

Grace Embraced

Then King David sent and brought him from the house of Machir the son of Ammiel, at Lo-debar. And Mephibosheth the son of Jonathan, son of Saul, came to David and fell on his face and paid homage. And David said, "Mephibosheth!" And he answered, "Behold, I am your servant." And David said to him, "Do not fear, for I will show you kindness..."

2 Samuel 9:5-7 (ESV)

Nature study at school was always interesting, especially since I had the added advantage of living in the countryside. Each week we would collect many new plants from the hedgerows, search for their names and "show and tell" the class. I think our fascination lay mostly with the very weird names which were allocated these wild plants. For example, who thought up the names 'bird's-foot trefoil', 'Jack-go-to-bed-at-noon', 'robin-run-the-hedge', 'common St John's-wort' and 'greater bladderwort'?

Flicking through the Bible there are a number of rather unusual names too, but none less than the mouthful 'Mephibosheth'. Mephibosheth was the son of Jonathan and grandson of Israel's King Saul. The boy was only five years old when his father and grandfather were killed in battle. Upon hearing the news of these events, the nurse in care of Mephibosheth hurriedly fled for a place of safety with the young child, and in her anxious effort, accidentally dropped him and crushed his ankles. Thus he was lame in his feet. In 2 Samuel 9, we read of how David rescued him from a hopeless situation and forever changed his life. Not only had Mephibosheth suffered the consequences of a fall, we are told that he was in the house of "Machir" in a place called "Lo-debar". Both the house and the place describe his condition. The Hebrew word used here for house literally means 'a prison'. The same word was used of Joseph when he was put in prison. Machir means 'sold', while Lo-debar means 'no pasture'. It was a place characterised by barrenness, a wasteland, no greenery. We get the picture. He had suffered the consequences of a fall and was now in a place where he felt imprisoned, sold and without hope.

However, keep reading because grace was extended to him. David desired to extend grace to a member of Saul's family and Mephibosheth was fetched. David called him by his name: "Mephibosheth!" The king said to him, "Do not fear, for I will show you kindness..." Mephibosheth had done nothing to merit the royal favour but he willingly embraced the grace that was offered to him and he was promised, "You shall always eat at my table."[45]

There is a lot of *me* in Mephibosheth. I too have suffered as a result of a Fall. I was in a place of Lo-debar. I had done nothing to merit royal favour but the King sought me and called me by name. He extended His grace to me and granted me perpetual fellowship and communion saying, "You shall always eat at my table." Have you embraced the same grace extended to you?

---

[45] 2 Samuel 9:7 (AMP)

13

Don't Get Discouraged

...Strength! Courage! Don't be timid; don't get discouraged.
God, your God, is with you every step you take.

Joshua 1:9 (MSG)

George Frideric Handel (1685-1759) is regarded as one of the greatest composers of all time. He composed popular works such as *Water Music, Music for the Royal Fireworks* and *Messiah*. After studying music in Germany and Italy, Handel moved to England at the age of twenty-seven, where he stayed for the rest of his life, becoming a composer for the Royal Chapel. His greatest passion was for the opera – an ill-timed passion, for the form was quickly falling out of fashion in England. Still, Handel continued to pen operas into the 1740s, losing more and more money. When his friends expressed concern that the concert halls were nearly empty, Handel responded that an empty venue meant great acoustics! In 1737 Handel's opera company went bankrupt and he suffered a stroke. His first oratorio, *Esther*, was condemned by church leaders for allowing the Word of God to be spoken in a theatre! By 1741 Handel was financially bankrupt, in great physical pain and the victim of several plots to sabotage his career.

Deeply depressed and facing a debtor's prison, Handel was visited by his friend Charles Jennens. The wealthy, devout Anglican had written a libretto about the life of Christ and the work of redemption, with the text completely taken from the Bible. Would Handel compose the music for it, he asked. Handel willingly agreed and estimated its completion in a year. He began composing *Messiah* on 22 August 1741. He composed the entire 260 pages in only twenty-four days, hardly leaving his room and rarely eating his meals. When he had finished writing what would become known as the 'Hallelujah Chorus', he exclaimed, "I did think I did see all Heaven before me, and the great God Himself." The premiere of *Messiah* on 13 April 1742, to an over-capacity crowd of seven hundred, was a sensation. The demand for tickets was so great that men were asked not to wear their swords, and women not to wear hoops in their skirts, to allow a hundred extra people into the audience.

If you are going through a difficult time, take courage. The next page of your life story has not yet unfolded. Strength! Courage! Don't be timid; don't get discouraged. God, your God, is with you every step you take.

14

God's Private Number 333

Call to Me and I will answer you, and I will tell you great and mighty things, which you do not know.

Jeremiah 33:3 (NKJV)

What an incredible promise! "Call to me and I will answer you..." This invitation was first made to Jeremiah. But it is extended to us as well. God says to Jeremiah, and through Jeremiah to us, "Call to me." The word "call" in Hebrew, *qara*, means 'to call forth and properly address by name'. It is a fervent expression of faith in God and trust in His goodness and power to act on your behalf. Remember, we are calling on the Great I AM!

The Amplified Bible says that God will "...show you great and mighty things, fenced in and hidden, which you do not know (do not distinguish and recognise, have knowledge of and understand)"[46]. He will help us figure out things we couldn't figure out for ourselves.

The secret [of the sweet, satisfying companionship] of the Lord have they who fear (revere and worship) Him, and He will show them His covenant and reveal to them its [deep, inner] meaning.

Psalm 25:14 (AMPC)

*The LORD is near to all who call upon Him,
  To all who call upon Him in truth.
He will fulfil the desire of those who fear Him;
  He will also hear their cry and will save them.*

Psalm 145:18-19 (NASB)

He's not aloof and uncaring. He's not too busy running the universe to help us. The Psalmist makes full use of this privilege:

---

[46] Jeremiah 3:33 (AMPC)

*Because He has inclined His ear to me, therefore I shall call
upon Him as long as I live.*

Psalm 116:2 (AMPC)

The Lord is inclined to help us.

"Because he loves me," says the LORD, "I will rescue him;
I will protect him, for he acknowledges my name.
He will call on me, and I will answer him;
I will be with him in trouble,
I will deliver him and honor him.
With long life I will satisfy him
and show him my salvation."

Psalm 91:14-16 (NIV)

Let's call on Him and be encouraged with the words of Psalm 138:

On the day I called, You answered me;
You made me bold with strength in my soul.

Psalm 138:3 (NASB)

15

Wisdom from Above

*But the wisdom that comes from heaven is first of all pure;
then peace-loving, considerate, submissive, full of mercy and
good fruit, impartial and sincere.*

James 3:17 (NIV)

*I*n chapter 3:13 James asks us to ponder a question, "Who is wise
and understanding among you?" No one wants to be seen as
foolish or unwise. We all want to be perceived as intelligent and
'in the know'. In verse 17 James shows us exactly what wisdom from
above looks like and how to personalise it in our lives.

Solomon writes:

*How blessed is the man who finds wisdom
And the man who gains understanding.*

Proverbs 3:13 (NASB)

Finding and applying *true* wisdom is very important to each and every
one of us. When Jesus told Nicodemus in John 3:3 that he must be "born
again"[47], He literally said "born *from above*" using the same word as
that in our verse today. Those born again / from above should operate in
wisdom from above, not earthly wisdom. James unflatteringly described
earthly wisdom in verses 14-15:

*But if you harbour bitter envy and selfish ambition in your
hearts, do not boast about it or deny the truth. Such "wisdom"
does not come down from heaven but is earthly, unspiritual,
demonic.*[48]

In contrast James presents us with seven characteristics or word
pictures of godly wisdom: pure, peace-loving, considerate, submissive,
full of mercy and good fruit, impartial and sincere.

---

[47] NKJV
[48] NIV

May

Two kinds of wisdom – and the evidence is in the fruit. Are you wise? Are you wise according to the world's ways or according to God's will? Do you employ the world's wisdom or do you follow godly wisdom from above?

16

His Very Great and Precious Promises

He has given us His very great and precious promises.

2 Peter 1:4

*N*otice that Peter not only describes the promises as being "great", but "very great"; he tells us they are "precious" and that God has given them to us.

Think of their Source. The source of any promise is very important, but when God makes a promise, we can be absolutely sure He will honour His word. We may make a promise and have every intention of keeping it, yet we may be prevented through no fault of our own. But there are no conceivable circumstances which can prevent God from honouring His word of promise. When God makes a promise, it is based upon His sovereignty and His character.

Think of their size. God's promises are described as "very great". The Greek word is *megistos*, the superlative of *megas*. Since *megas* means 'great', you can picture the idea inherent in the superlative *megistos*, which means greatest, exceedingly great or preeminent. The KJV says He has "given unto us exceeding great and precious promises". God, the Source "is able to do exceeding abundantly above all that we ask or think"[49] and "is able to make all grace abound"[50] toward us. When we consider the content of God's promises and the great blessing they offer, then at once we see how very great they are. He not only gives us peace but the promise of *perfect* peace.[51] He not only promises His forgiveness but He will *remember our sins no more.*[52] He not only gives us life but the promise of life *to the full.*[53]

---

[49] Ephesians 3:20 (KJV)
[50] 2 Corinthians 9:8 (NKJV)
[51] See Isaiah 26:3; cp. Philippians 4:7
[52] See Jeremiah 31:34
[53] See John 10:10

Think of their significance. He has given these precious promises to us. We are the recipients. The previous verse states that He has given us "everything we need for a godly life"[54]. There is such provision in these precious promises. God has given us His promises – and in them He has given us everything we are going to need for time and eternity. John Bunyan, who spent much of his life in a prison cell, came to know well these precious promises of God and wrote:

> *The pathway of life is strewn so thickly with the promises of God that it is impossible to take one step without treading upon one of them.*[55]

Can you think of a biblical promise which is very special to you? Remember 2 Corinthians 1:20:

> *For no matter how many promises God has made, they are "Yes" in Christ. And so through him the "Amen" is spoken by us to the glory of God.*

> *2 Corinthians 1:20 (NIV)*

---

[54] 2 Peter 1:3 (NIV)
[55] John Bunyan; *The Pilgrim's Progress*

17

Christian – a Rich Saint

For in Him you have been enriched in every way.

1 Corinthians 1:5 (NIV)

n anagram is a word or phrase made by transposing or rearranging the letters of another word or phrase. For example:

- Dormitory = Dirty room
- Eleven plus two = Twelve plus one
- Listen = Silent
- Clint Eastwood = Old West action
- Madam Curie = Radium came
- The countryside = No city dust here
- Astronomers = Moon starers
- The eyes = They see
- The Morse code = Here come dots
- A decimal point = I'm a dot in place

Here's an interesting one: Christian = rich saint. A Christian is enriched with every spiritual blessing in Christ[56] and declared to be complete in Christ.[57] Paul refers to these blessings as "the unfathomable riches of Christ"[58]. "Unfathomable" is the Greek *anexichniastos* which conveys the idea that the believer's blessings in Christ are 'too deep to be measured'. We often think of enrichment as applying to one's economic realm, but God's view is far more expansive and includes "every way". The Living Bible (TLB) says, "He has enriched your whole life."

Our riches are outlined clearly in Ephesians 1. In fact, when Paul outlines them, he exuberantly explodes in praise and in the original Greek

---

[56] See Ephesians 1:3
[57] See Colossians 2:10
[58] Ephesians 3:8 (NASB)

this is clearly seen, as verses 3-14 are all one long sentence! It has more than two hundred words. He then prays for us in verse 18:

> *I pray that the eyes of your heart may be enlightened, so that you will know what is the hope of His calling, what are the riches of the glory of His inheritance in the saints, and what is the surpassing greatness of His power toward us who believe.*
>
> *Ephesians 3:18-19 (NASB)*

May we be enlightened and freshly appreciate the great riches that Christ brings to the table of our lives.

18

Stay Connected

I am strong for all things in the One who constantly infuses strength in me.

Philippians 4:13 (Wuest)

God understands the very core of our being and the wiring of our lives; He made us, after all. He knows when we are overloaded and about to blow a fuse. He understands when our energy runs on empty and our emotions short-circuit. He is the One who can switch currents from negative to positive and transform our thoughts. He is the All-powerful One, the Alpha and Omega, who can flow into the capacitor of our lives, generate supernatural strength and step up our lives to fulfil His purpose. Let's not insulate ourselves from His power to help or resist His loving hand. It's all about staying connected and allowing God's power to freely flow in and through our lives!

Putting today's verse in context, Paul was speaking of "the secret of being content in any and every situation"[59] and the secret lay in connection with Christ. He is the One who infuses strength in us and helps us persevere.

In conclusion, be strong in the Lord [draw your strength from Him and be empowered through your union with Him] and in the power of His [boundless] might.

Ephesians 6:10 (AMP)

The word "strong" means 'to be empowered; to be strengthened'. Be empowered through your union with Him. The connection is vital; it is "through ... Him" and "in the Lord." Jesus stated:

---

[59] Philippians 4:11 (NIV)

May

> *"I am the vine. You are the branches. He who remains in me, and I in him, the same bears much fruit, for apart from Me you can do nothing."*
>
> *John 15:5 (WEB)*

Our greatest need as believers is to stay deeply connected with Christ. Take time today to appreciate your connection and allow Him to freely flow, infusing you with fresh strength.

19

The Counsel of the Lord

For who has stood in the counsel of the LORD,
And has perceived and heard his word?
Who has marked his word, and heard it?

Jeremiah 23:18 (NKJV)

A few verses after the one above, God says, "I have not sent these prophets, yet they ran. I have not spoken to them, yet they prophesied. But if they had stood in My counsel, and had caused My people to hear My words, then they would have turned them from their evil way and from the evil of their doings."[60] Did you notice the words "stood in the counsel of the Lord" and "stood in My counsel"? These false prophets which were addressed failed to stand in the counsel of the Lord. Like those rebuked in Psalm 106:13, "They did not wait for His counsel."[61] When we fail to wait on God's counsel (daily reflecting on His love, faithfulness, purposes and resources), we quickly lose our focus, and in a spirit of idolatry and human foolishness we begin to strategise in self-effort to get what we think we need for our happiness, security and satisfaction.

Where do we source our counsel each day? In Psalm 1 we see God's prescription for blessedness. It opens with the very words, "How blessed is the man who does not walk in the counsel of the wicked."[62] The whole psalm shows the difference between walking in the counsel of the ungodly versus walking in the ways of God. To achieve the latter, we need to take time to meditate on His Word day and night (or stand in His counsel). The psalmist stated:

Your statutes are my delight; they are my counselors.

Psalm 119:24 (NIV)

---

[60] Jeremiah 23:21-22 (NKJV)
[61] NKJV
[62] Psalm 1:1 (NASB)

God gently reminds us:

I will instruct you and teach you in the way you should go;
I will counsel you with my loving eye on you.

Psalm 32:8 (NIV)

What a verse! Take time now to ponder it and personalise it until it becomes practical in your life. Chew on it and digest it until it is assimilated into your system and disseminated throughout your very personality.

Let's not hesitate to draw close to the One who is our Wonderful Counsellor[63] and allow Him to help us navigate the issues of life. Allow him to counsel you with His loving eye upon you.

---

[63] See Isaiah 9:6

20

Dawn is About to Break

But make sure that you don't get so absorbed and exhausted in taking care of all your day-by-day obligations that you lose track of the time and doze off, oblivious to God. The night is about over, dawn is about to break. Be up and awake to what God is doing! God is putting the finishing touches on the salvation work He began when we first believed. We can't afford to waste a minute, must not squander these precious daylight hours in frivolity and indulgence, in sleeping around and dissipation, in bickering and grabbing everything in sight. Get out of bed and get dressed! Don't loiter and linger, waiting until the very last minute. Dress yourselves in Christ, and be up and about!

Romans 13:11-14 (MSG)

Think back over this past week. How much of what you did was motivated by your conscious awareness of the coming of the Lord? We often get so caught up with daily duties and deadlines that we forget the big picture. We forget that Jesus is coming and that we should be living each day in light of that great future event. Not only is this not a time to be "oblivious to God", but it is, in fact, a time to put God first and foremost in our lives. The time for lingering is over. It is time to be up and awake to what God is doing. The alarm went off hours ago!

Don't just lolly gag around. Don't sleepwalk through life in a sedated state of existence. Someone said to me recently, "My days were a blurred haze of busy." I can relate to that honest evaluation and it is all too easy to get so absorbed and exhausted in taking care of all our day-by-day obligations. We forget that "the dawn is about to break" and that we are here on purpose for such a time as this. We have a mission to fulfil, a message to share and mercy to show to those suffering around us. We are not meant to be frivolously frittering away on time on our every whim or fruitlessly fighting one another. These are purposeful days and, as our verse states, "we must not squander these precious daylight hours".

Theodore H. Epp wrote:

> *Live as though Christ died yesterday, rose from the grave today, and is coming back tomorrow.*

That puts it all in perspective for me. I encourage you to take time to ponder that profound sentence and allow the Cross, the resurrection and the Coming of Christ to shape your thinking.

Today, I challenge myself to "dress in Christ" and be "up and about"! Will you do the same?

21

God's Great Grip

So do not fear, for I am with you;
  do not be dismayed, for I am your God.
I will strengthen you and help you;
  I will uphold you with my righteous right hand ...
For I am the LORD your God
  who takes hold of your right hand
and says to you, Do not fear;
  I will help you.

Isaiah 41:10,13 (NIV)

A long time ago the English rock band known as the Beatles crooned the refrain, "I want to hold your hand." When our children were small, we would enjoy holding hands even if it was just a simple stroll in the garden or along the beach. The intimacy was comforting and reassuring. However, when we were in town and came to a busy road or a crowded area, holding hands took on a different meaning. I would clamp down on that little hand with all my parental love and protection. While I would say, "Hold on tight," and the little hand would grasp my hand tightly, I would never depend on their grasp. It was I who held my child's hand in a firm grip.

The Psalmist stated:

  ...you hold me by my right hand.

Psalm 73:23 (NIV)

What a great thing to know in times of trouble and weakness that being safe isn't dependent on our grip. Being safe is dependent on God's grip.

God tells us, "Do not fear," because:

- "I am with you."
- "I am your God."
- "I will strengthen you."

- "I will help you."
- "I will uphold you."

Rest today in His grip which reassures and calms, protects, steadies and upholds us.

22

Cracked Christians

For my people have committed two evils:
They have forsaken Me, the fountain of living waters,
And hewed themselves cisterns – broken cisterns, that can hold
no water.

Jeremiah 2:13 (NKJV)

Yesterday evening I watched a French drama entitled *Jean de Florette*, which is set in the rustic environment of Provence in the 1920s. It starts with the enterprising Ugolin returning to his native countryside after serving in the military. Intent on a lucrative business of growing carnations, he conspires with his uncle Cesar to gain access to a hidden spring on a neighbouring property. When their initial attempt to buy the land fails, they contend with Jean de Florette, who arrives with his family to work the coveted plot and turn it into a profitable farm. Relying on cisterns, the family soon run out of water and watch their crops fail. All the time a wonderful secret spring of fresh water was there for them.

Jeremiah used the imagery of a cistern and spring in chapter two. In Bible lands, a cistern was an artificial reservoir which was dug in the earth or hewn in the rock for the collection and storage of water. But the cisterns would often develop leaks and dry up. It didn't make sense for people to depend on old, broken cisterns when right beside their cistern there was a continuous spring of living water. This was a picture of the people of Israel. They laughed at Jeremiah's metaphor, but in reality they were laughing at themselves because they had rejected the true God who was called "the spring of living water"[64]. Imagine yourself as a very thirsty person in a parched land, turning away from a bubbling spring of cool water to hack out a cistern in the dirt, under the parched sun, in the hopes of collecting some rainwater! Why would anyone place their trust

---

[64] Jeremiah 2:13 (NIV)

in the unstable, unfulfilling cisterns of earth when they can place their trust in a stable, satisfying God? Seems like such a no-brainer – yet don't you and I sometimes fall into that trap? We dig our own cisterns – broken cisterns – and expect them to satisfy our thirst and bring us contentment. We drink from the broken cisterns of materialism, position, wealth, popularity, etc...

> *Jesus said ... "Everyone who drinks this water will be thirsty again, but whoever drinks the water I give them will never thirst. Indeed, the water I give them will become in them a spring of water welling up to eternal life." The woman said to him, "Sir, give me this water so that I won't get thirsty and have to keep coming here to draw water."*
>
> *John 4:13-15 (JBP)*

In John 7 we are told, Jesus Christ the Living Water stood and said in a loud voice, "Let anyone who is thirsty come to me and drink. Whoever believes in me, as Scripture has said, rivers of living water will flow from within them." This was such an important invitation, Jesus said it in a loud voice. Did you catch that? Do you hear it in your heart right now? Come to Him and drink.

> *As the deer pants for streams of water,*
> *so my soul pants for you, my God.*
> *My soul thirsts for God,*
> *for the living God.*
>
> *Psalm 42:1-2 (NIV)*

23

The Perfected Expresso

I press on to take hold of that for which Christ Jesus took hold of me. Brothers and sisters, I do not consider myself yet to have taken hold of it. But one thing I do: Forgetting what is behind and straining toward what is ahead, I press on toward the goal to win the prize for which God has called me heavenward in Christ Jesus.

Philippians 3:12-13 (NIV)

Most days I assemble with the coffee community in my locale for my beloved beverage, an Americano. Walking in, you are embraced by the robust smell of coffee in the air, dim lighting and familiar hipster décor. Perusing the menu, you soon find that there is a flavour for everyone, a style for every lifestyle. High on the list of popularity in Europe is the espresso. An espresso is made in a machine which 'presses' steam 'outwards' through tightly packed dark roasted coffee beans.

We talk of expressing juice from grapes or expressing milk from cows. We talk about expressing an opinion where we verbalise the thoughts which press through our brains and become vocal through our mouths. 'Express' has now also come to mean 'for one particular purpose'. For example, a letter can be sent by express delivery. An express train avoids irrelevant stops and takes you expressly to your particular destination. The express lane in the supermarket checkout allows you a speedy exit.

When Paul wrote to the Philippians, He told them that he too had one particular purpose and he was pressing on to achieve it. "But one thing I do," he said. "I press on toward the goal." Wrapped up in the word "press" *(dioko)* is the idea of pressure. Occurring three times in Philippians 3:4-14, it means 'to follow', 'to pursue', suggesting impassioned pursuit, earnestness and diligence.

In the 1992 Olympic games held in Barcelona, one of the greatest candidates for the gold medal in the 400-metre run was British athlete

Derek Redmond. However, early in the race his dreams were shattered when he felt his hamstring go. Instead of stopping, he began to hobble around the rest of the track, determined to finish. Limping painfully down the course, he remained intent on finishing the race, no matter how long it took. As the other runners sped by, a figure pushed his way out of the stands and onto the track. Redmond's father put his arm around him, lifted his son's arm over his shoulder, and helped him to finish the race. The image of father and son crossing the finishing line became a defining one for the 1992 Olympics. For us it is a marvellous illustration of God's enormous mercy and grace when failure or brokenness besets us on the path toward our goal. If we will just stay on track, we can go the distance, because we have a heavenly Father who will come, put His arms around us, undergird us and see us through to the end. When the pressure is on, press on!

24

Spoiler Alert

And we know that in all things God works for the good of those who love him, who have been called according to his purpose.

Romans 8:28 (NIV)

Under 'A Diagnostic Guide to Reading' I noticed a poll which posed the question, "While you're reading a book, have you ever skipped ahead to read the ending?" Well, how would you answer? I had to honestly answer yes because I am one of those people who can't read a book without flicking to the end to check what's going to happen. Astonishingly, 60% (or rather 59.52%) replied yes as well, with the remaining 40% saying no. A remarkable number admitted to reading the ending first on a regular basis, maintaining that they did not mind spoilers, and they stated that knowing where a book was heading actually enhanced their reading enjoyment.

Let me pose another question. "Have you ever read a book and then gone to watch it in the cinema?" Imagine you are sitting comfortably in your seat when the music suddenly heightens everyone's senses. It comes to the part where something threatening happens. Those around you gasp at the crisis on the screen. You, however, remain poised with popcorn in hand. Why? You have read the book. You know the ending.

Recently I was watching a DVD with my family at home and I must admit that after about twenty minutes I Google-searched how it all panned out! Since I knew the ending (I didn't tell anyone), I was no longer agonising over the hero's fate. So now I could enjoy the camera angles, musical score and scenery in a whole new way. In fact, even when things became tense, I could relax and enjoy, since I knew the finish. I had knowledge of the end of the movie, so whatever happened beforehand, I was at peace.

God has the eternal perspective on your life. He views things from an eternal angle. He knows "the end from the beginning"[65].

> *"For I know the plans I have for you," declares the LORD, "plans to prosper you and not to harm you, plans to give you hope and a future."*
>
> *Jeremiah 29:11 (NIV)*

God views your life with confidence. We know that in all things God works for the good of those who love Him. Enjoy the journey and stay poised with peace.

---

[65] Isaiah 46:10 (NKJV)

25

Chain Reaction

About midnight Paul and Silas were praying and singing hymns to God, and the other prisoners were listening to them. Suddenly there was such a violent earthquake that the foundations of the prison were shaken. At once all the prison doors flew open, and everyone's chains came loose. The jailer woke up, and when he saw the prison doors open, he drew his sword and was about to kill himself because he thought the prisoners had escaped. But Paul shouted, "Don't harm yourself! We are all here!" The jailer called for lights, rushed in and fell trembling before Paul and Silas. He then brought them out and asked, "Sirs, what must I do to be saved?" They replied, "Believe in the Lord Jesus, and you will be saved – you and your household."

Acts 16:25-31 (NIV)

So much is said here in this selection of Scripture. Many dramatic descriptions are deployed such as, "At once all the prison doors flew open," "everyone's chains came loose," and the powerful words of the jailer, "…what must I do to be saved?" A lot is going on, but I want to direct your attention to verse 25. It says that Paul and Silas were praying and singing hymns to God – but check out the last eight words: "…and the other prisoners were listening to them."

The word "listening" is the Greek verb *epakroaomai*. This verb is rarely used in the New Testament; it means 'to listen intently'. They hung on every word.

In their darkest hour, at midnight, in the deepest part of the dungeon, Paul and Silas decided to pray and praise God. They could have spent their time complaining. We would have understood. The other prisoners probably would have chimed in in agreement. But instead, they used their mouths to bring honour to God. The accents of praise to God swept through the confines of the cell. Not only did the other prisoners hear them but their prayers and praise infiltrated the throne room of God. Then we read, "At once all the prison doors flew open and everyone's chains came loose."

From this very episode sprang the nucleus of the Philippian church. Whatever your prison is today, realise that there are others listening to your words and response; others who are going through trials who need hope and encouragement. Regardless of your circumstances, people are listening to you, and God is listening as well. Let's let our light shine in this world and let others see the true glory of God in our lives. Someone once said:

> *As long as you pout and murmur about the darkness, about the mistreatment, about the injustice, midnight will dominate, but as you pray and praise then midnight will dissipate.*

26

Sailing on S.S. Tarshish

"Arise, go to Nineveh, that great city, and call out against it, for their evil has come up before me." But Jonah rose to flee to Tarshish from the presence of the LORD. He went down to Joppa and found a ship going to Tarshish. So he paid the fare and went down into it, to go with them to Tarshish, away from the presence of the LORD.

Jonah 1:2-3 (ESV)

At the age of twelve I boarded the SS Uganda for my first school trip. It was to be an educational cruise and indeed we visited various cities. But I do recall the Bay of Biscay, those little brown paper bags, and trying to sleep in the dorms on a hammock down in the former cargo area of the ship. Two years after my trip the SS Uganda was called up for military service and became a hospital ship. Jonah also boarded a ship, as we see from our above verse.

"Arise" is an invitation to join God in what He is doing! Jonah was invited to carry out two specific things: first, go to Nineveh; second, call out against it – that is, rebuke them for their sin and call them to repentance. "But Jonah," the first two words of verse 3, are the saddest words in the whole book. Jonah did just the opposite of what God wanted. Nineveh was about 550 miles east of Jonah. Tarshish was 2,500 miles west. We are told that he went down to Joppa, where he found a ship bound for that port. Disobedience is always downward, never upward. As you read the full chapter you can see the downward digression from God. God tells him to "arise" but Jonah chooses to go down. First he went down to Joppa. Then he went down into the ship. Then down into the sea, then down into the fish's belly, then down into the deep. When you choose to leave the sure path of God's will, you begin a long downward trail that leads to disaster.

Running from God is a downward trip. It is also expensive. You get to pay the fare. There is a high price for a Tarshish trip and a high price for disobedience, as it takes us from the presence of God.

As chapter one progresses, we see that Jonah has boarded a ship heading in the opposite direction from the will of God for his life. Then a storm comes up which threatens not only Jonah but the rest of the crew as well. His disobedience affected others. We too impact others by our choices and behaviour. Rebellion has a ripple effect. Jonah was running from God's Word and God's will for his life. How about us? What is God saying to you personally today through His Word?

27

God is For Us

What, then, shall we say in response to these things? If God is for us, who can be against us?

Romans 8:31 (NIV)

A popular idiom states, "All roads lead to Rome." This was literally true in the days of the Roman Empire when all the empire's roads radiated out from the capital city, Rome. When it comes to Christian theology, we could say that just about all roads lead through Romans. Paul's letter to the Romans is such a profound book and chapter 8 is perhaps its greatest section, referred to by some as "the summit of the summit". As we ascend to verses 31 to 39, we reach the climactic section, of which Mounce declared:

Nowhere in the annals of sacred literature do we find anything to match the power and beauty of this remarkable paean of praise.

The word "if" which Paul uses in verse 31 does not denote doubt but is a conclusion, a consequence or an affirmation signifying 'since'. The argument is this: God is so evidently for us that nothing or no-one can successfully be against us.

You can sleep in a den of lions and you can walk through a fiery furnace. You can bring down your Goliath. You can have your meal barrel full of oil in the middle of famine.

In Psalm 59 David was on a rollercoaster of emotions. By verse 9 he had regained his footing, attained the right perspective and confidently stated:

This I know, that God is for me.

Psalm 56:9 (NASB)

With this conviction thoroughly fixed in his mind, he could moderate his anxieties and calmly await God's deliverance.

Again, in Psalm 118 he said:

> The LORD is for me; I will not fear;
> What can man do to me?

Psalm 118:6 (NASB)

God is for us. Earlier in the book of Romans Paul told us:

> But God shows His love for us in that while we were still
> sinners, Christ died for us.

Romans 5:8 (ESV)

To say that God is for us means that everything in God's sovereign plan, his redemptive acts and the situations in our lives have been and always will be in accordance with His love for us.

Embrace this truth today knowing that God is for you.

28

The Saggy Old Cloth Cat

The heart of man plans his way,
but the LORD establishes his steps.

Proverbs 16:9 (ESV)

Bagpuss was a children's television programme not to be missed in our house. The title character was known as "a saggy, old cloth cat, baggy, and a bit loose at the seams".

The first two minutes, fifty-one seconds of each programme was identical.

Through a series of sepia photographs, we were introduced to a little girl named Emily who owned a shop. Emily found lost and broken things and displayed them in the window so that their owners could come and collect them; the very unusual shop did not sell anything. She would leave the object in front of her favourite stuffed toy, the large, saggy, pink and white striped cat named Bagpuss. As soon as Emily left the room, Bagpuss would wake up. The programme shifted from sepia to colour and various toys in the shop came to life. Bagpuss and his motley crew of Madeline the ragdoll, Gabriel the toad and pompous professor Yaffle and the mice would discuss and mend the new-found object. Then Bagpuss would start yawning again, and as he fell asleep the narrator would speak as the colour faded back to sepia. A simple plot with much repetition.

In later years I learned that Bagpuss was an actual cloth cat but was not intended to be such an electric pink. It should have been a ginger marmalade moggy but the company Dunbar Fabrics in Folkestone responsible for dyeing the material made a mistake and it turned out pink and cream. "It was the best thing that ever happened," said Firmin the show's creator. Whilst the company offered to replace the fabric, Firmin decided to stick with it and it was the colour of Bagpuss which wooed so many fans, the original Bagpuss now being a firm fixture in Canterbury Heritage Museum, together with other characters and Emily's shop window.

Sometimes life's events do not turn out as we have planned. God knew that Joseph's brothers would throw him into a deep pit and sell him to traders on their way to Egypt. What Joseph's brothers meant for evil, God intended for good. Joseph said:

"God meant it for good, to bring it about that many people should be kept alive, as they are today."

Genesis 50:20 (ESV)

In the last years of her life, Corrie ten Boom, author of *The Hiding Place* and honoured for her work in sparing the lives of Jewish people from the Nazis, often began her testimony by holding up before the audience a piece of embroidered cloth. First she showed the beauty of the embroidered side with all the threads forming a beautiful picture, which she described as God's plan for our lives. Then she would flip over the cloth to show the tangled and confused underside, illustrating how we so often view our own lives from a human standpoint. God always knows what's best for us, 100% of the time. God sees around the proverbial corner of time and knows the plans He has for us. Even when the fabric of life seems to be unravelling, trust God and allow Him to work all things for good.

29

The Sound of a Ticking Clock

Look carefully then how you walk, not as unwise but as wise, making the best use of the time, because the days are evil.

Ephesians 5:15 (NIV)

I'm told that a pup may cry for a number of reasons, but one common reason is the absence of his mother's heartbeat. The rhythmic sound of a heartbeat is calming for young pups. Apparently, placing a ticking clock in his bed is one way to help stop your little fur baby from crying.

Does the sound of a ticking clock soothe you or really tick you off? Having grown up in a house full of clocks which chimed every fifteen minutes and cuckooed on the hour, I never really noticed the impact of a clock until... I purchased a wall clock for my office. This clock looked impressive and practical as it had five individual faces displaying the time of different worldwide cities. The issue arose when I inserted the batteries and discovered not only an unbearably loud ticking sound but none of them ticked at the same time... Each clock seemed allergic to synchronism and kept ticking like a mighty metronome. Needless to say, it drove our household crazy. The batteries were removed, time stopped and peace prevailed.

However, in life, time cannot be controlled. We all equally get twenty-four hours in a day and no-one is short changed. As songwriter Chris Rice once wrote:

Every day is a bank account, and time is our currency. No one's rich, nobody's poor – we get 24 hours each.

While we may idiomatically talk of trying to 'find time', it is elusive. Even though you can't control time, you can control how the time you have is used. Wise people realise that time is a precious commodity. Paul tells us, a sign that a person is wise is that he is sensitive to how he uses his time; he makes a disciplined use of his time. Wisdom is the art of spending time wisely.

Have you ever considered the time investment in some of the world's greatest achievements? It took Da Vinci four years to paint the *Mona Lisa*. It took Michelangelo four years to paint the ceiling of the Sistine Chapel. It took Leo Tolstoy over six years to write *War and Peace*. It took ten years for Victor Hugo to write *Les Miserables*. It took thirty-six years to build St Paul's cathedral. It took Noah a hundred years to build the ark. This list reminds me of just what can be accomplished when a person consistently channels their energy and time wisely. Inscribed on a sundial are the words, "It is later than you think." Seize the day. Make it count for God and leave your footprints on the sands of time.

30

The Irish Daisy

I planted the seed, Apollos watered it, but God has been making it grow. So neither the one who plants nor the one who waters is anything, but only God, who makes things grow.

1 Corinthians 3:6-7 (NIV)

While known as the Irish daisy, it's most popular name is the dandelion. Have you ever wondered how the dandelion got its name? The coarsely-toothed leaves of the common dandelion have been said to resemble a lion's teeth. In French, this is roughly translated as *'dent de lion'*, a term which we have corrupted to create the moniker we know today. It's scientific name *Taraxacum* originates from the Greek words *taraxos*, meaning 'disorder', and *akos*, meaning 'remedy'. Its species name, *officinale*, derives from the Latin *officinalis*, which roughly translates as 'of pharmaceutical value'. The French word for dandelion is *pissenlit*, which translates 'to pee the bed'. Dandelions are indeed a good diuretic and in fact they are as strong as some of the commercial products. Up until the 1800s people would pull grass out of their lawns to make room for dandelions because they knew that every part of the dandelion was useful: root, leaves, flower. It can be used for food, medicine and dye for colouring.

If you've ever lived in an area in which the dandelion grows, it's likely that you've cusped a dandelion in your hand and blown the dried seeds of the flower into orbit. Once dandelions turn from their vibrant golden yellow colour to an intricate white globe of geometric genius and gossamer delicacy, they can be blown, dispersing the seeds into the air like tiny parachutes. When each seed blows through the air, it eventually lands somewhere, where it will likely form a new dandelion plant. I'm told that a flower head can produce up to four hundred seeds but the average is 180. A plant may have a total of two thousand to twelve thousand seeds. in its lifetime. The seeds are often carried as many as five miles from their origin.

Jesus tells us in Luke 8 that the seed is the Word of God and our responsibility is to be a sower of that seed and scatter the seed bountifully. Let us spread the good news of God's love to everyone and trust Him for the growth.

31

Nature's Velcro

They brought back word to them and to all the congregation, and showed them the fruit of the land. And they told him, "We came to the land to which you sent us. It flows with milk and honey, and this is its fruit. However, the people who dwell in the land are strong, and the cities are fortified and very large. And besides, we saw the descendants of Anak there."

Numbers 13:26-28 (ESV)

*I*n 1968, Puma became the first major shoe company to offer a pair of trainers/sneakers with Velcro fasteners. Other companies caught on and by the 1980s, many children seemed to own at least one pair of those three-strap Velcro wonders. I, for one, am so grateful for this product. Velcro is the brainchild of Georges de Mestral, a Swiss engineer who, in 1941, went for a walk in the woods on a lovely summer's day and was struck by the tenacity with which burrs clung to the hair of his dog and the wool of his socks. He wondered if the burrs which clung to his trousers – and dog – could be turned into something useful. Under a microscope, he found at work the hook-and-loop principle on which Velcro is based. After nearly eight years of research (apparently, it's not so easy to make a synthetic burr), de Mestral successfully reproduced the natural attachment with two strips of fabric, one with thousands of tiny hooks and another with thousands of tiny loops. He named his invention Velcro, a combination of the first syllables of velvet and crochet. The latter word is French for 'hook'. While the invention was a success, it didn't really take off until the 1960s, when NASA's extensive use of Velcro in space came to the public's attention. Since then, the hook and loop fastener has stuck with us, and its popularity shows no sign of ever falling off.

Like Georges de Mestral, I too had many walks in the countryside with my dog, a West-highland terrier, and the same type of burrs had also stuck to my dog's coat. However, I looked on it as a nuisance as I painstakingly had to pick each burr off by hand. Isn't it interesting how we can see things differently? What do you see that others don't?

The Bible often asks the question, "What do you see?" I have always enjoyed the story of Moses sending the twelve spies from the twelve tribes of Israel when they were on the verge of entering the Land of Canaan. The Bible states that when they returned, they reported to Moses. They all saw the grapes which represented the potential and prosperity of the land. They also saw giants which represented problems! Since the Amalekites, who were the giants of the land, were spread out throughout the entire region, ten of the spies saw themselves as grasshoppers:

> *"We were in our own sight as grasshoppers..."*
>
> *Numbers 13:33 (WEB)*

However, two of the spies, Joshua and Caleb, saw God at work. They said:

> *"If the Lord delights in us, He will bring us into this land and give it to us, a land that flows with milk and honey."*
>
> *Numbers 14:8 (ESV)*

They all saw the grapes and giants. But only two saw God at work. What do you see that others don't? Faith sees the invisible, believes the incredible and receives the impossible.

What Shall I Read Next?

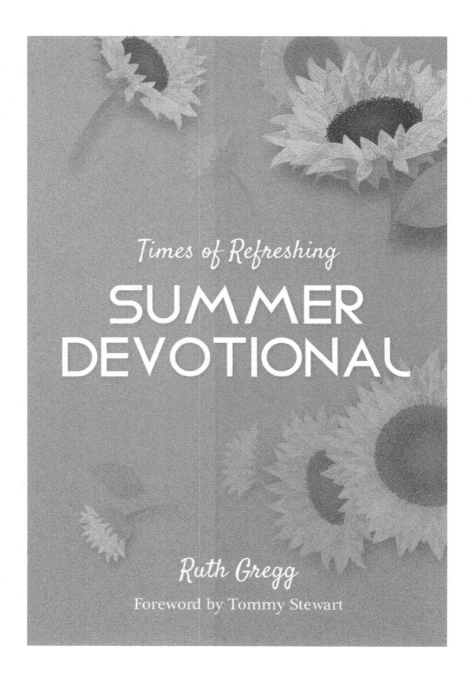

Times of Refreshing

SUMMER DEVOTIONAL

Ruth Gregg

Foreword by Tommy Stewart

Made in the USA
Monee, IL
13 October 2022

15793365R00109